I0393182

Pat Durbin Quilts

© 2017

Pat Durbin

A Walk in the Woods

Exhibited at the National Quilt Museum
April 14 – July 11, 2017

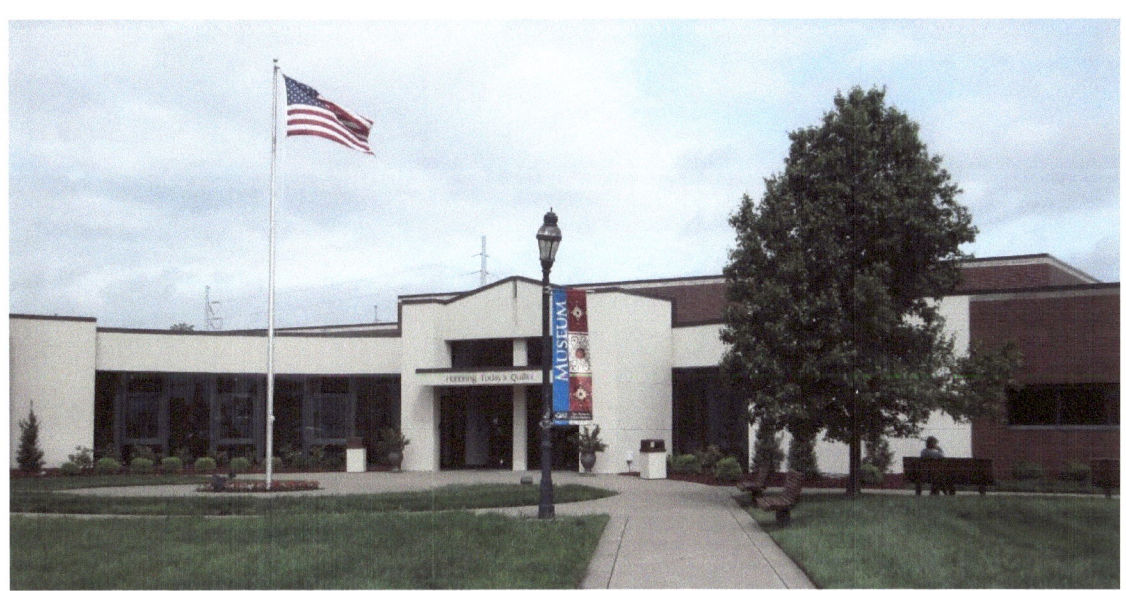

Dedication

Judy Schwender, curator of the National Quilt Museum.

Thanks for asking me.

Thanks to Gary, my husband, he's the "photo" part of this book...both before and after the quilt is made. Thank you Gary!

Always...my thanks go to God, for His many gifts and inspiration.

Acknowledgements

I've thought of doing a "Photo to Quilt" book many times. This is a sample.

Since I have been asked to do an exhibit at the National Quilt Museum, it seemed fitting to use those quilts included in the exhibit for this small book.

Photo-to-Quilts

Pat Durbin

Contents

Dedication/Acknowledgements	2
Quilts as Art	4
Inspiration Photos-to-Finished Quilts	
Among Giants	7
Azalea Lagoon	9
Lift Your Eyes to the Hills	11
Whispers of Hope	13
Sequoia Duckpond	15
Agate Beach	17
Inner Strength	19
Forest Walk	21
Come Sit With Me	23
Beside the Still Waters	25
Vanishing Homestead	27
Wild Rhodies	29
Smith River	31
Sunlight in the Forest	33
Cloudy Day at Hidden Lake	35
Begonia Picotee Lace	37
Rest Stop	39
Coastal Garden	41
Meet the Durbins	42

Quilts as Art –

As we step into the woods a feeling of awe comes over me. I notice the beauty of creation, light and shadow, the colors, smells and sounds. I become inspired to give thanks and maybe even to attempt an art quilt. I especially love driving through the redwoods with the sun shining—I never get tired of it.

You will see in my art many landscape scenes that have come from various trips we have made. We often pull to the side of the road and Gary, my husband, and I grab our cameras to try to capture a memory. I use these photos as guides to my quilts. When I'm ready for a new project I pour through the archives of photos for the spark of inspiration.

I love the beauty and warmth of quilted art. Most of my works are favorite landscapes and special people. The familiar medium of fabric and thread are my tools. I use them to build works of art that bridge the gap between fine art painting and traditional quilts. Although my techniques vary my needle consistently glides through the construction of all pieces.

It has been my joy to make things with fabric almost all of my life. I started sewing at about 4 yrs.—just simple stuff—which then became doll clothes, and then my own clothes. I continued to sew clothing for myself and my family for many years.

My Grandmother, Jennie, made quilts. I always loved to look at them but was reluctant to make them because all of hers were "hand-made". I'm sort of a get-it-done kind of sewer. So it wasn't until about 1993 that I finally gave myself permission to make quilts using my sewing machine.

My first quilts were traditional bed quilts, or kid quilts. I began using designs of my own, but they remained pretty traditional. It wasn't until I entered a quilt and then visited the American Quilter's Society show in Nashville (2004). There I saw that people were making art quilts and using unconventional methods in their work.

I went home with a whole new vision of what quilting could be.

I've always had this hidden desire to be an "artist"…that is paint pictures and so forth. It is not surprising that my first "art" quilts were representational…portraits of loved ones and then landscape scenes. Using fabric to make those desired pictures was just a natural progression of my gifts. I've spent a lot of time experimenting.

I developed a method I call, "Mosaic Picture Piecing", this method allows me to work on a scene in the approximate size it will be when finished…no need for seam allowances or difficult applique. You will see many examples of this type of work in the exhibit—sometimes in combination with other methods.

Other experimentation took me to painting on fabric. There are several quilts using that method shown here as well.

Another thing I've played with a lot is free motion thread embroidery. I started making these motifs in order to make my trees and bushes look more realistic. I've used this technique in a lot of different ways, which you will also see in several quilts.

It is my honor to have an exhibit here in the National Quilt Museum. I appreciate all of the work they do to advance the art of quilting.

I hope that you enjoy my quilted art. I've certainly enjoyed my journey of making the quilts.

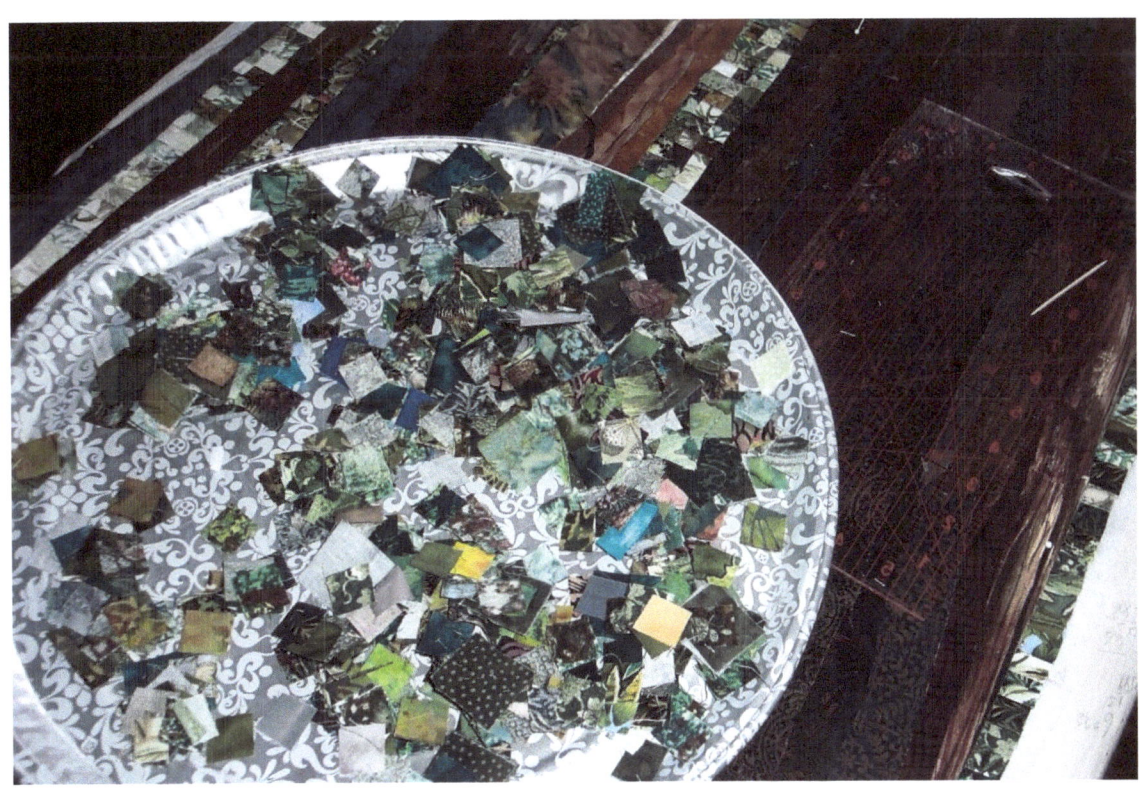

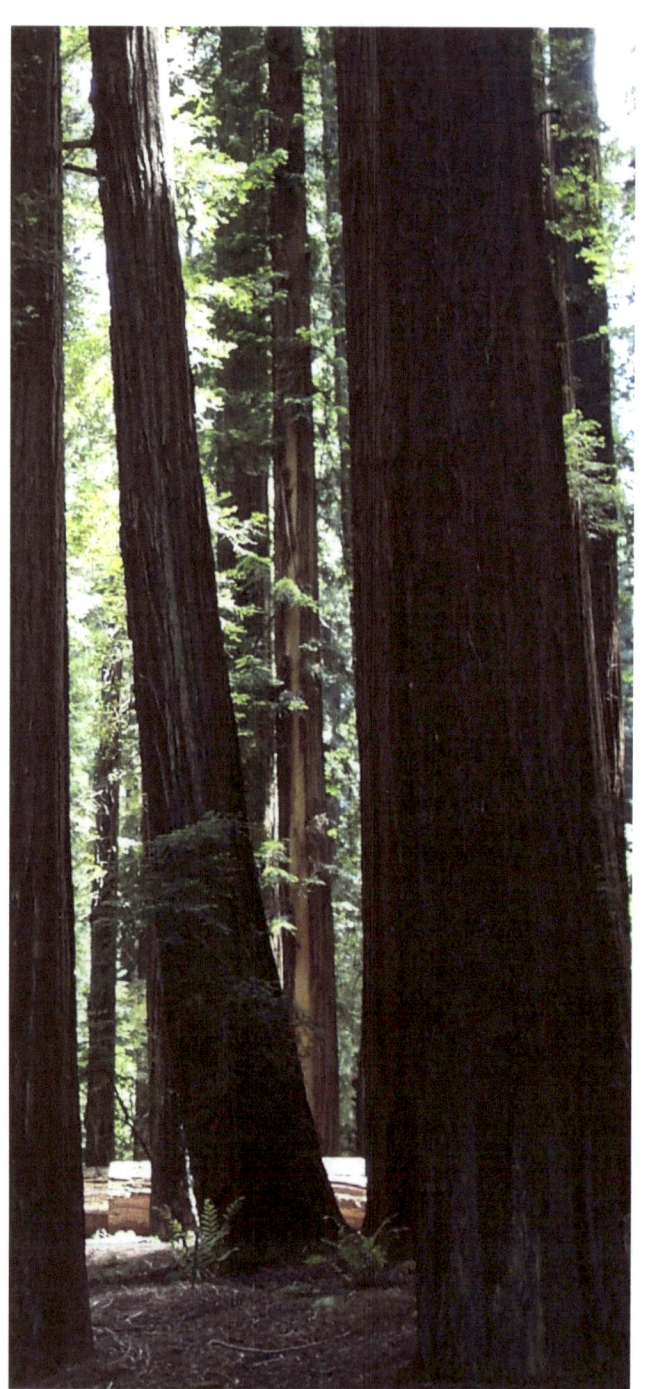

Inspiration photo Gary Durbin

AMONG GIANTS

43" x 86"

Walking through the redwood forest is always awe inspiring. I've loved these redwoods all of my life. One day we were at a wedding, the sun was shining and I asked my husband to take shots of the trees. This was the view I chose. I decided to do a narrow, tall quilt to help enhance the feeling of height. However, you'll never appreciate these grand giants unless you walk on the forest floor and feel the majesty and your own insignificance. I hope that by viewing the quilt, you get a glimmer of the "feel" of the redwood forest.

I used my Mosaic Picture Piecing technique with ½" squares of many cotton prints for the forest floor and the leafy backgrounds. The trees were formed with long strips of many fabrics to help imitate the long stringy bark of the redwoods. The baby redwood in the middle is constructed of thread. The ferns are fussy cut from a beautiful print. Batting is Warm cotton. The whole quilt is overlaid with a layer of black tulle netting and then the quilt is heavily machine quilted using free form designs.

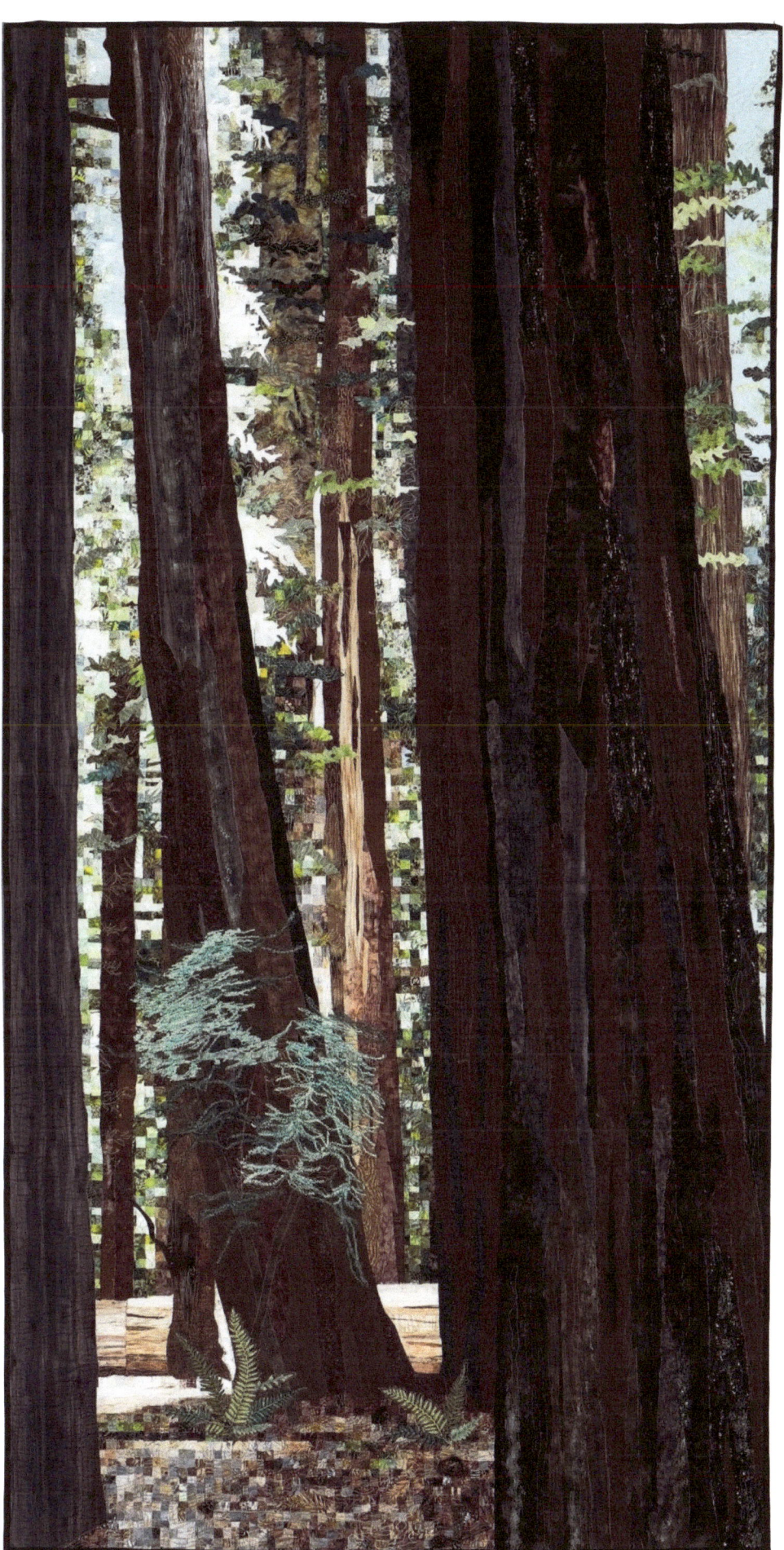

Among Giants

AZALEA LAGOON

60" x 24"

I grew up boating and enjoying Big Lagoon, on the North Coast of California. Just north of Big Lagoon is an Azalea park area. We enjoyed the view here and the peek back at the Lagoon.

The quilt has a combination of several techniques including painted flowers.

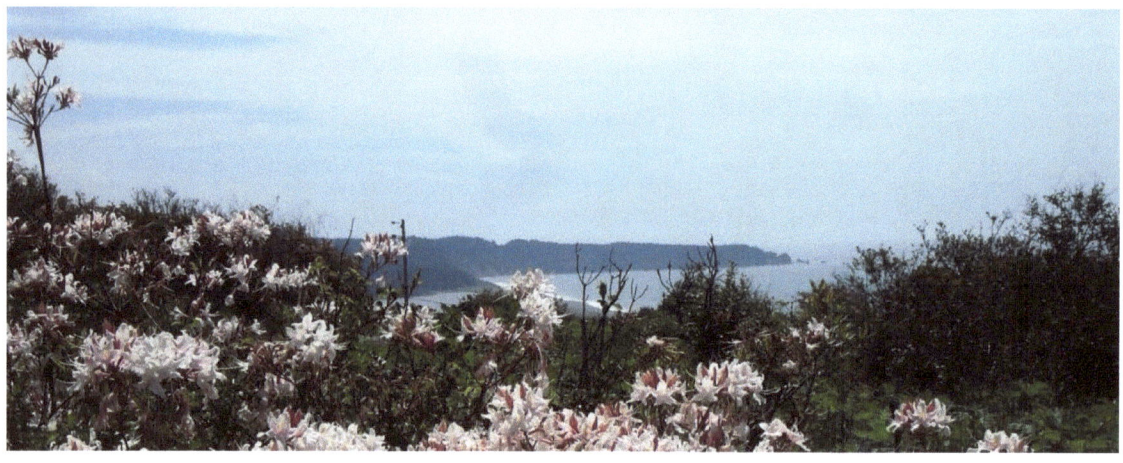

Inspiration photo Gary Durbin

Azalea Lagoon

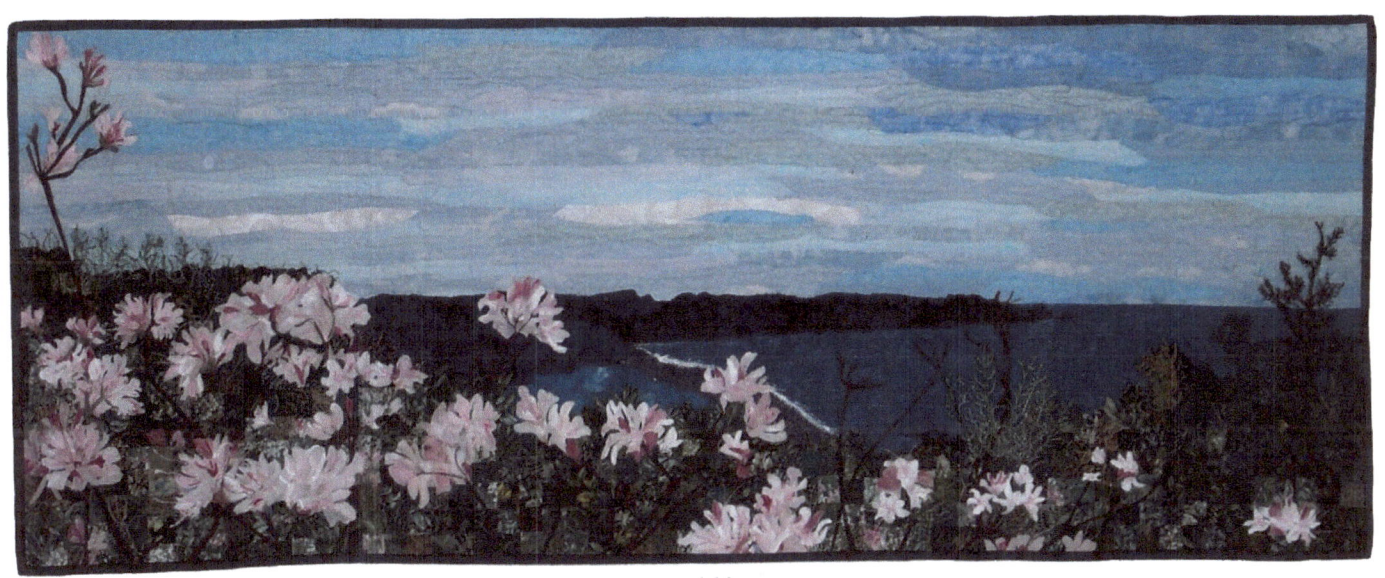

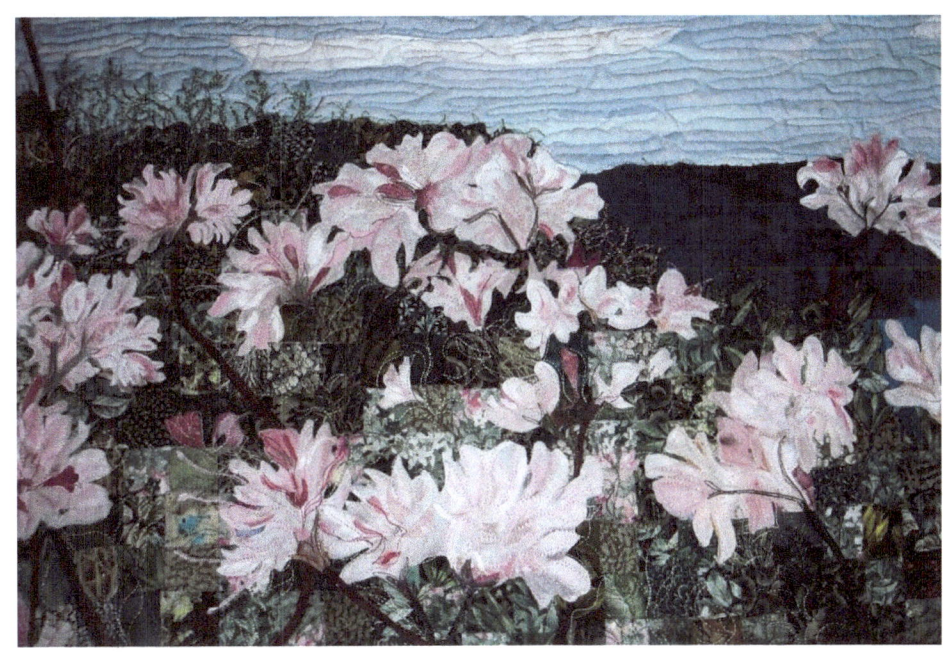

LIFT YOUR EYES TO THE HILLS   67" x 62"

Glacier National Park was our retreat trip as we grieved over the loss of our son in 2010. I will always remember him as I view this piece.

The Bible verse: "*I will lift up mine eyes unto the hills, from whence cometh my help. My help cometh from the Lord, which made heaven and earth.* Ps 121

Techniques: painted background, applique and embroidery, machine quilted

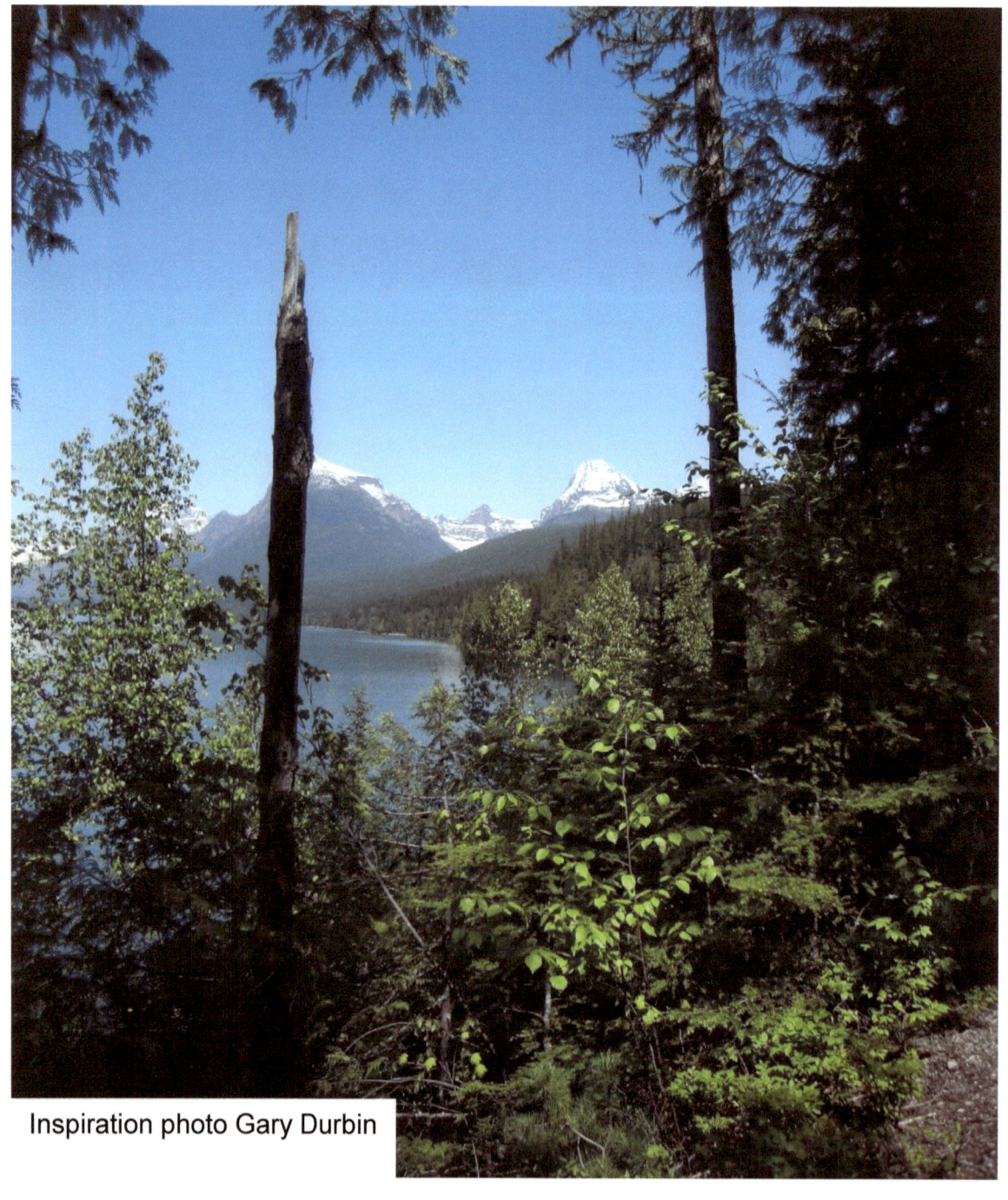

Inspiration photo Gary Durbin

Lift Your Eyes to the Hills

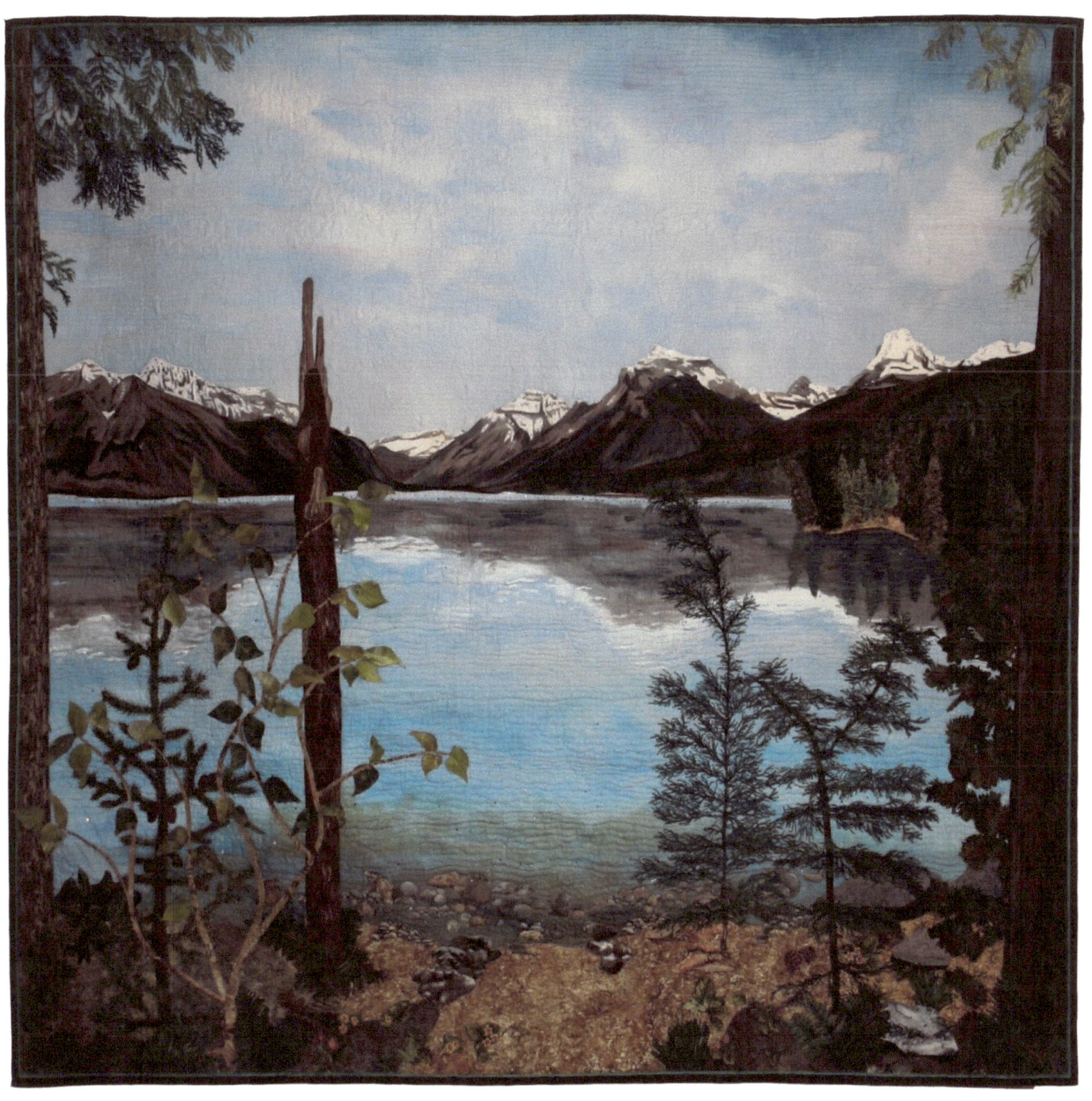

WHISPERS OF HOPE   52" x 44"

During Easter week our neighbors' tree sprang into glorious bloom. It reminded me of the Hope of the Resurrection. I was in my "thread play stage" so the pink part is all constructed of thread.

Techniques: Mosaic picture piecing, raw edge applique, touches of paint, crystals, heavy freehand machine embroidery and machine quilted with Superior Threads.

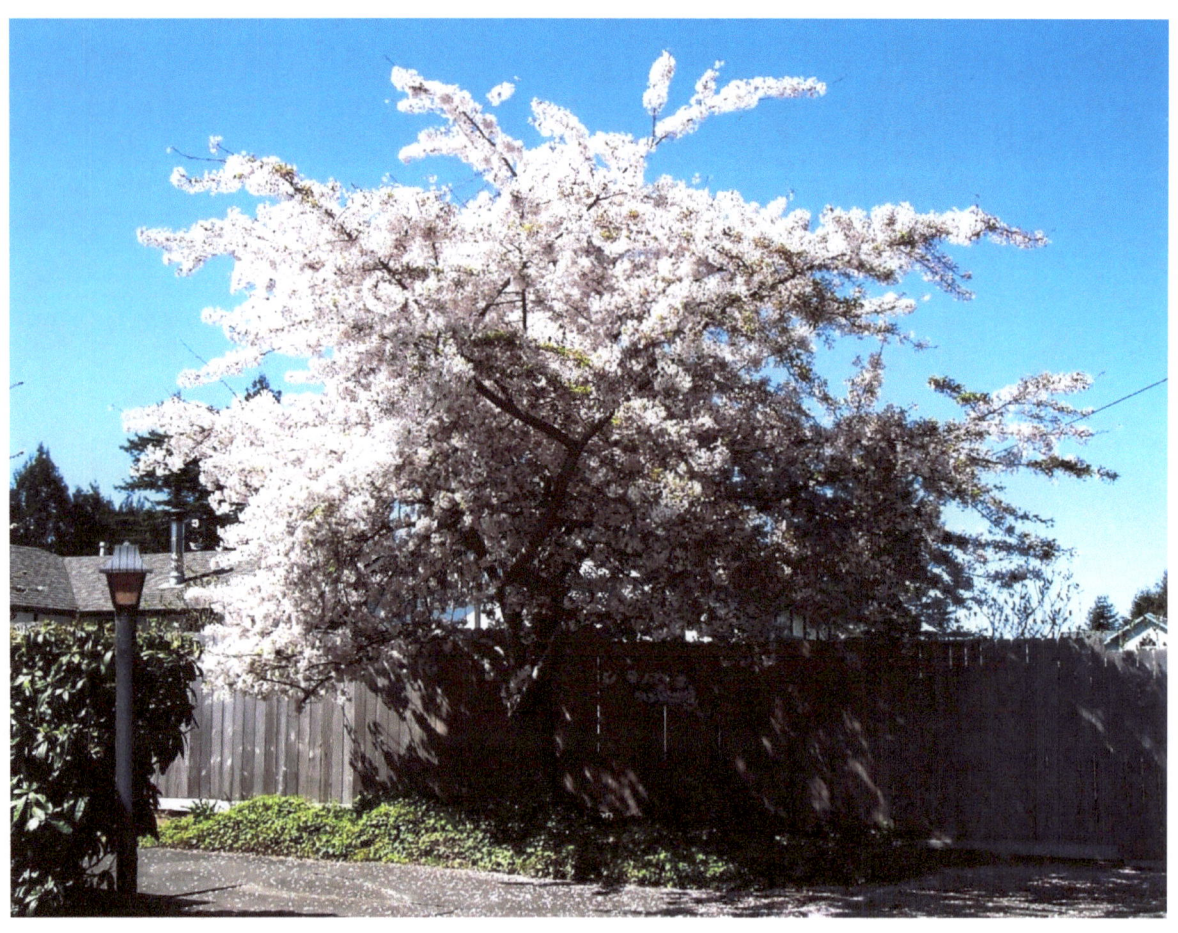

Inspiration photo Gary Durbin

Whispers of Hope

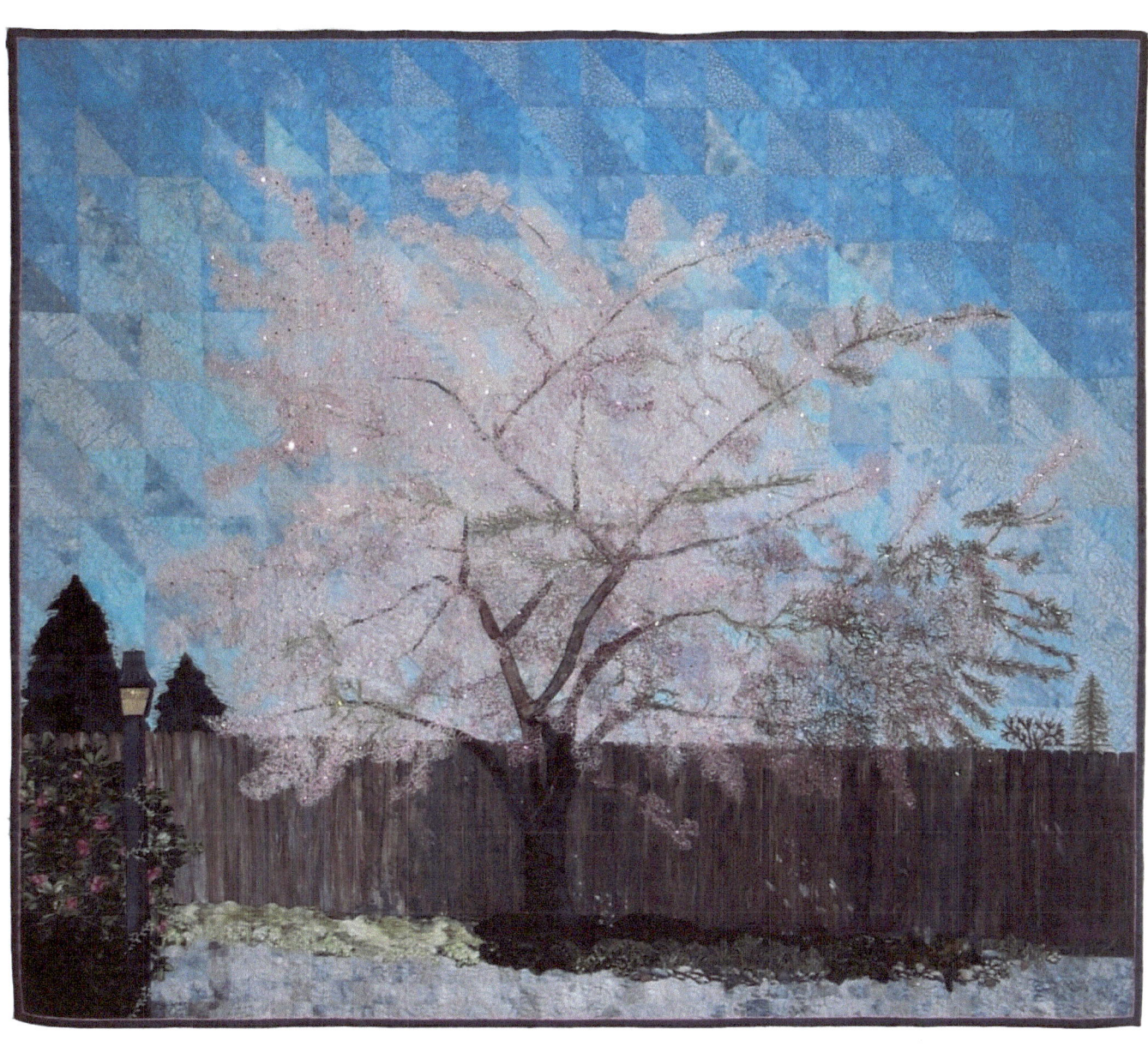

77" x 87"

Visiting the Duckpond in Eureka, Ca. has been a family activity for as long as I can remember. The quiet little pond surrounded by giant redwoods stirs memories and inspires.

Techniques: Mosaic Picture Piecing, applique, many different styles.

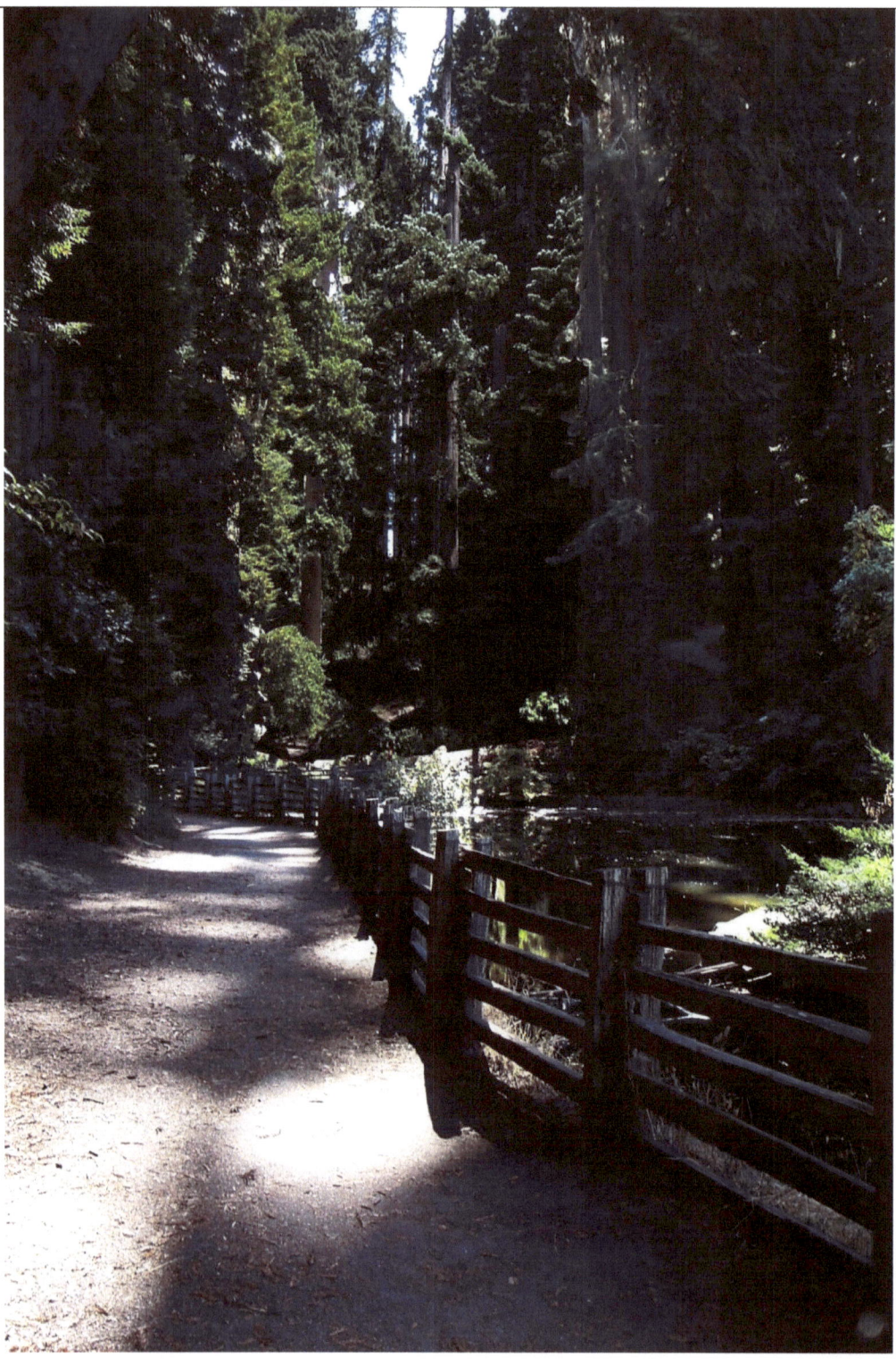

Sequoia Duckpond

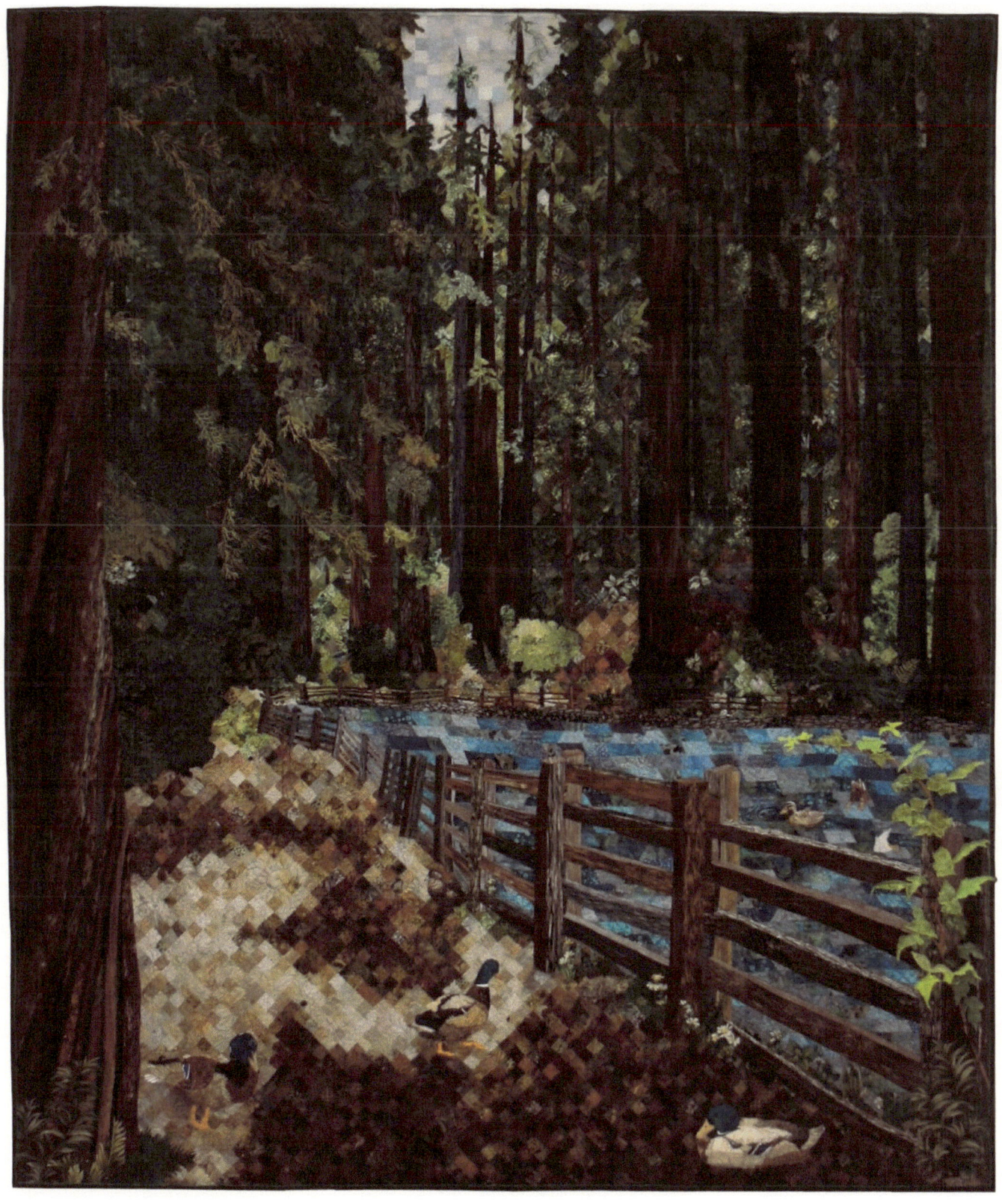

AGATE BEACH 60" x 40"

We often hunt agates on this beach called Dry Lagoon. Sometimes the wave action on the rocks really brings on some mighty splashes.

Techniques: Mosaic picture piecing, tulle overlay, tiny rocks, machine quilted.

*This is the very first quilt on which I tried the "Mosaic" method.

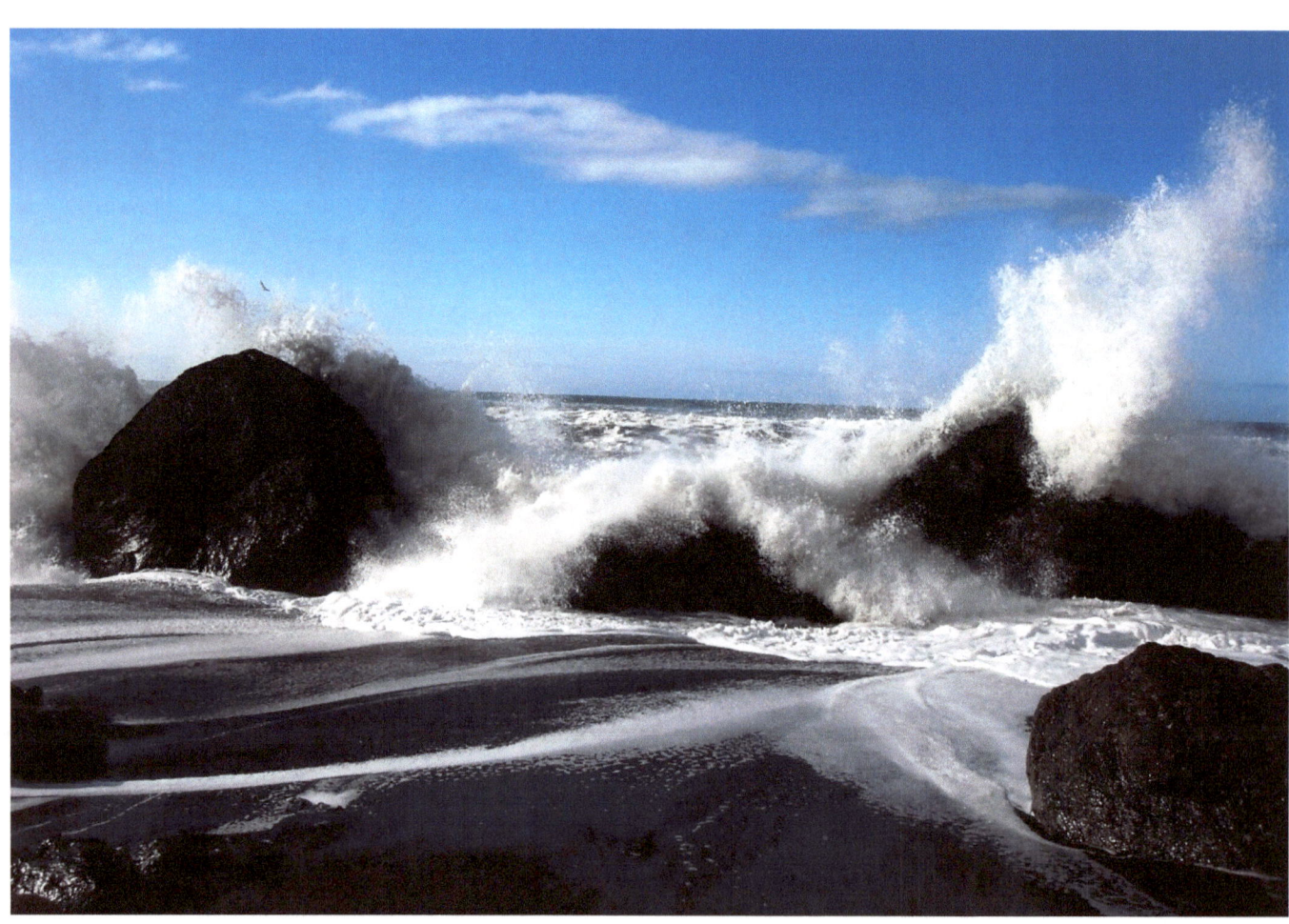

Agate Beach

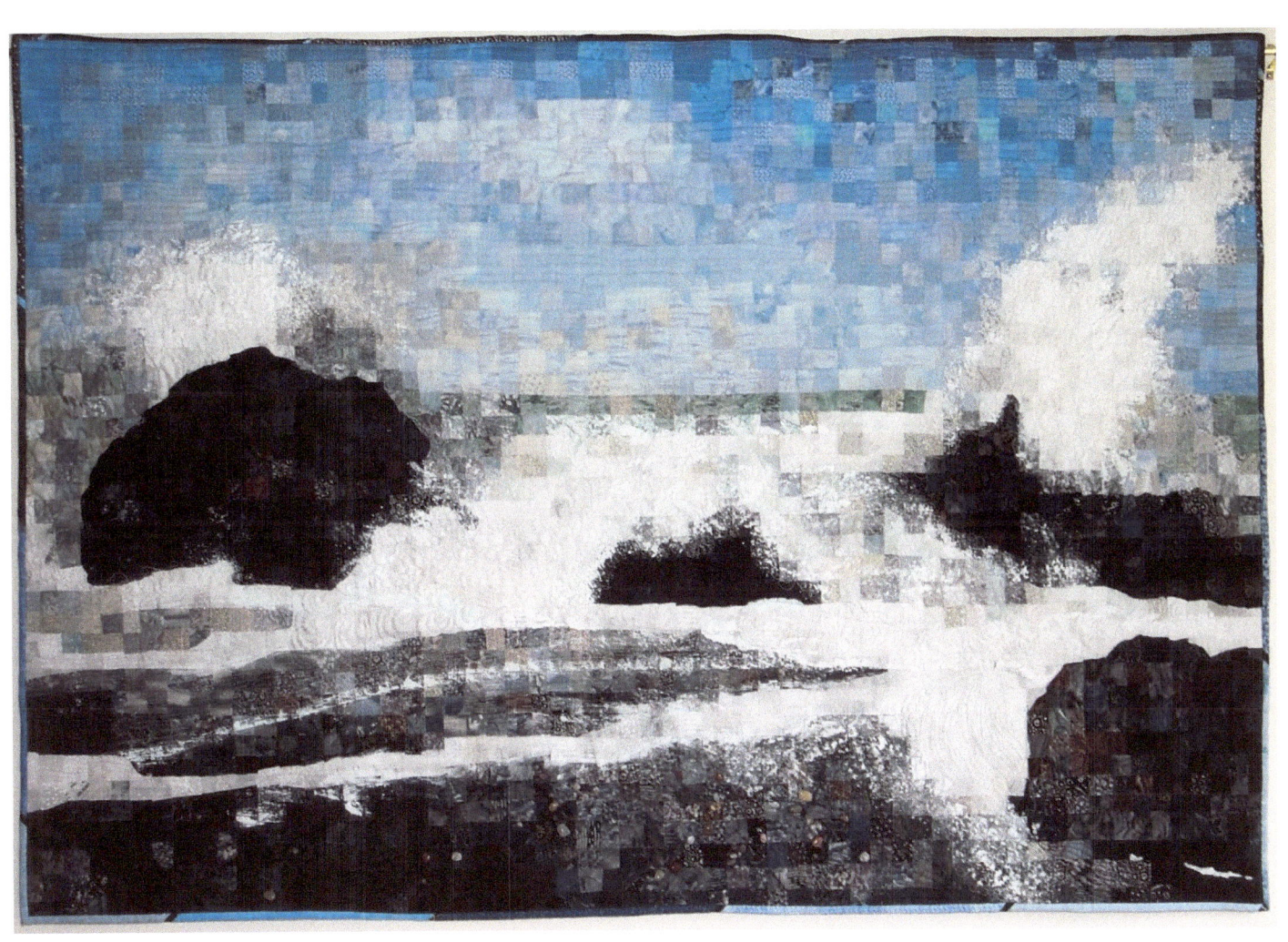

INNER STRENGTH   47" x 35"

My Fiber Art Friends decided on a quilt challenge of local bridges. This covered bridge near our home was my choice. I loved the architecture of the inside of the bridge and the view to the outside.

The quilt has a combination of several techniques including paint & dye.

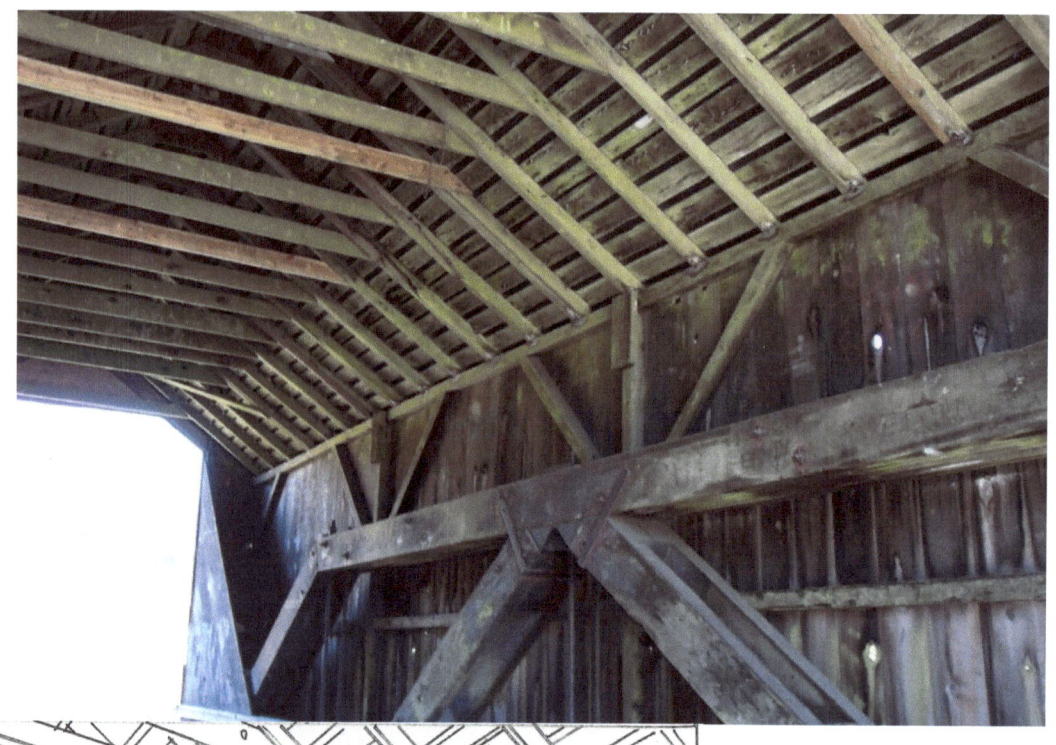

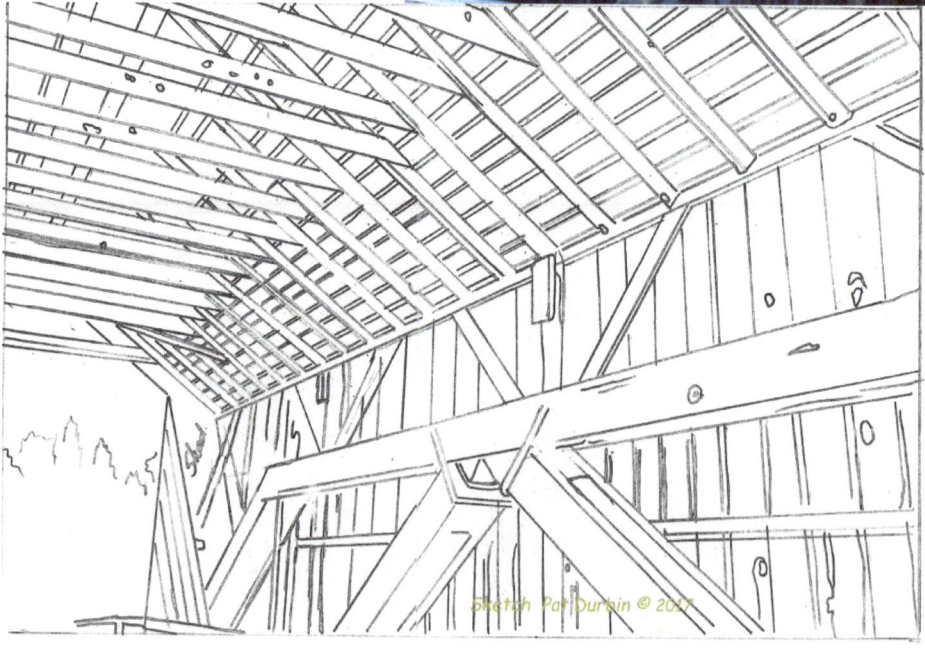

Inner Strength

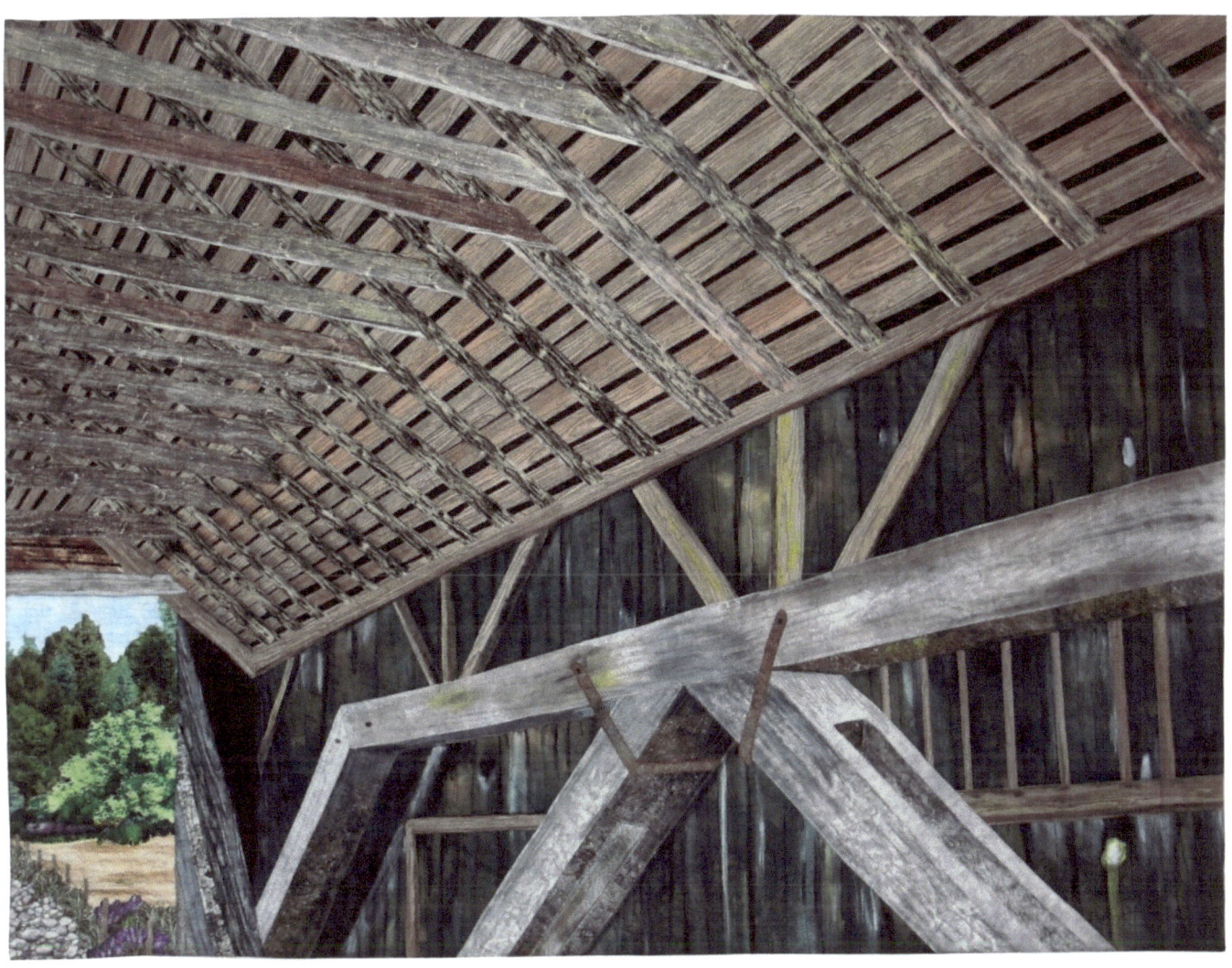

FOREST WALK   67" x 86"

I grew up in Arcata, Ca. and spent many good times climbing around and running the trails in this park. However, I had not been there in many years.

The park had changed from my memory. Now there is a beautiful walking trail from the lower entrance. So we began, and the walk was slow because we had to get so many pictures along the way. When I saw the stairway, inspiration hit!

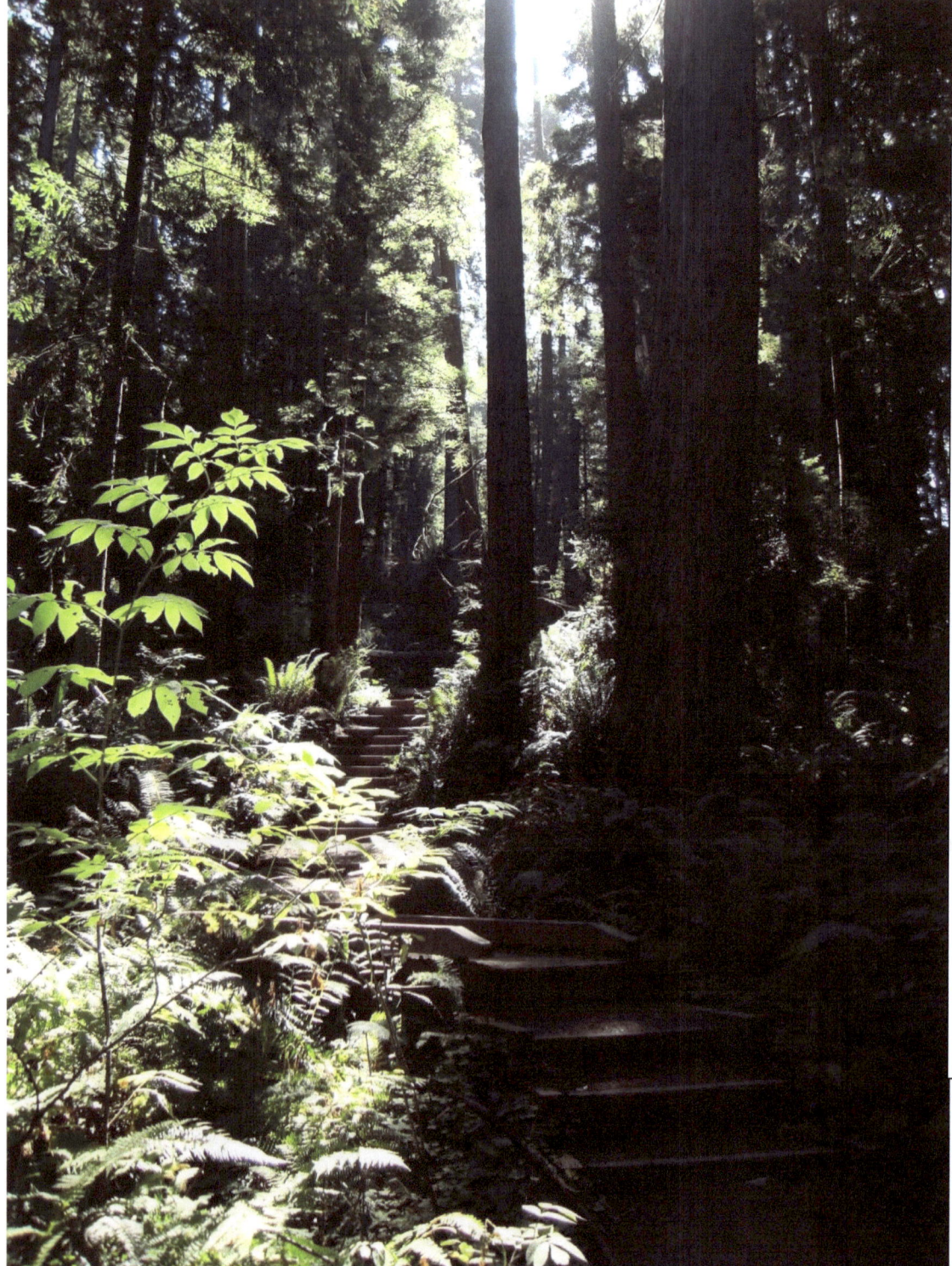

Forest Walk is now part of the permanent collection of the museum.

Forest Walk

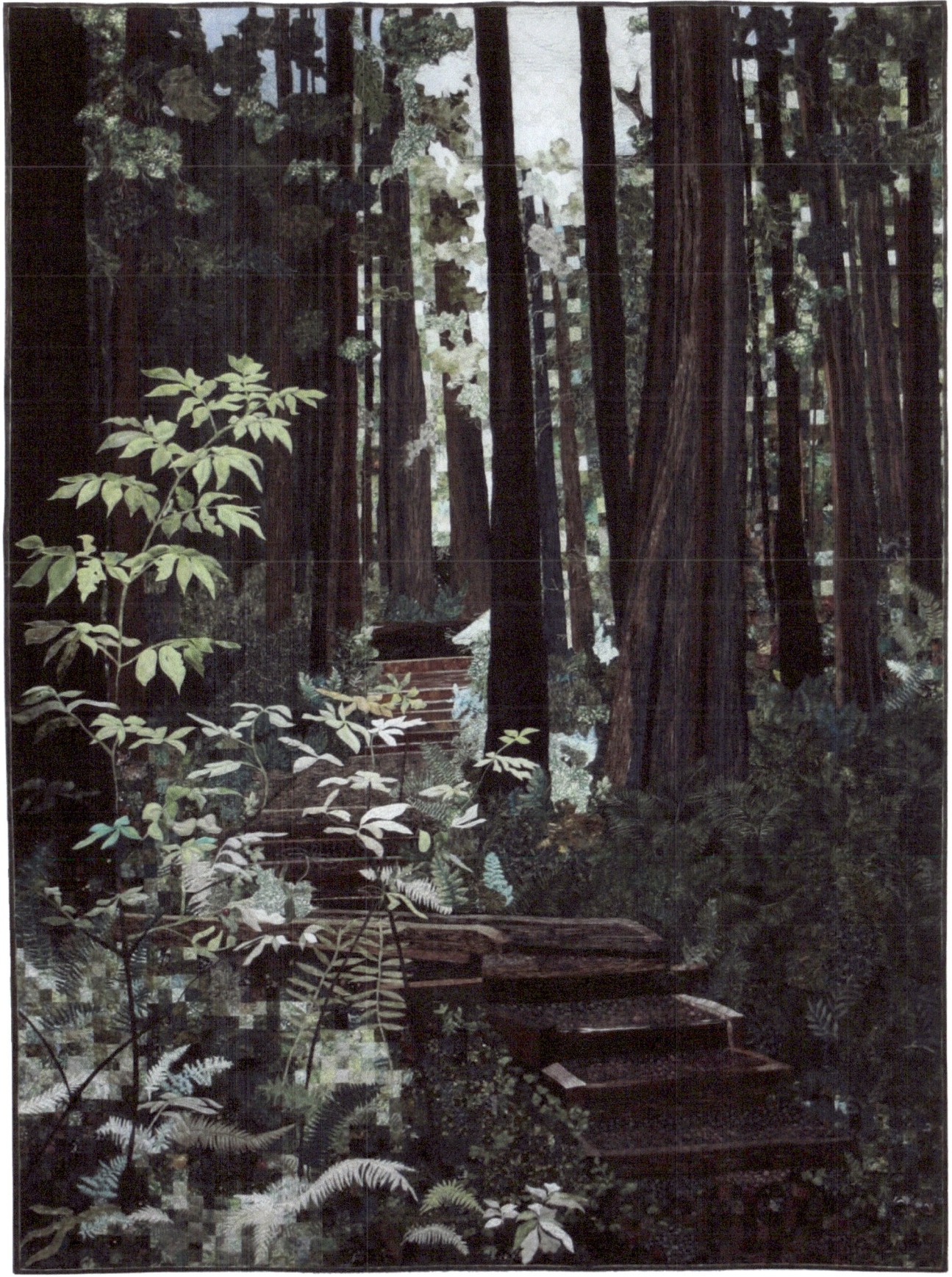

COME SIT WITH ME   42" x 34"

 Our adult kids came to join us at Paducah during the quilt show one year.
They rented a house on Kentucky Lake where we enjoyed a fun reunion.
This patio scene of the backyard warms my heart with memories.

Techniques: painted patio, applique, machine embroidery

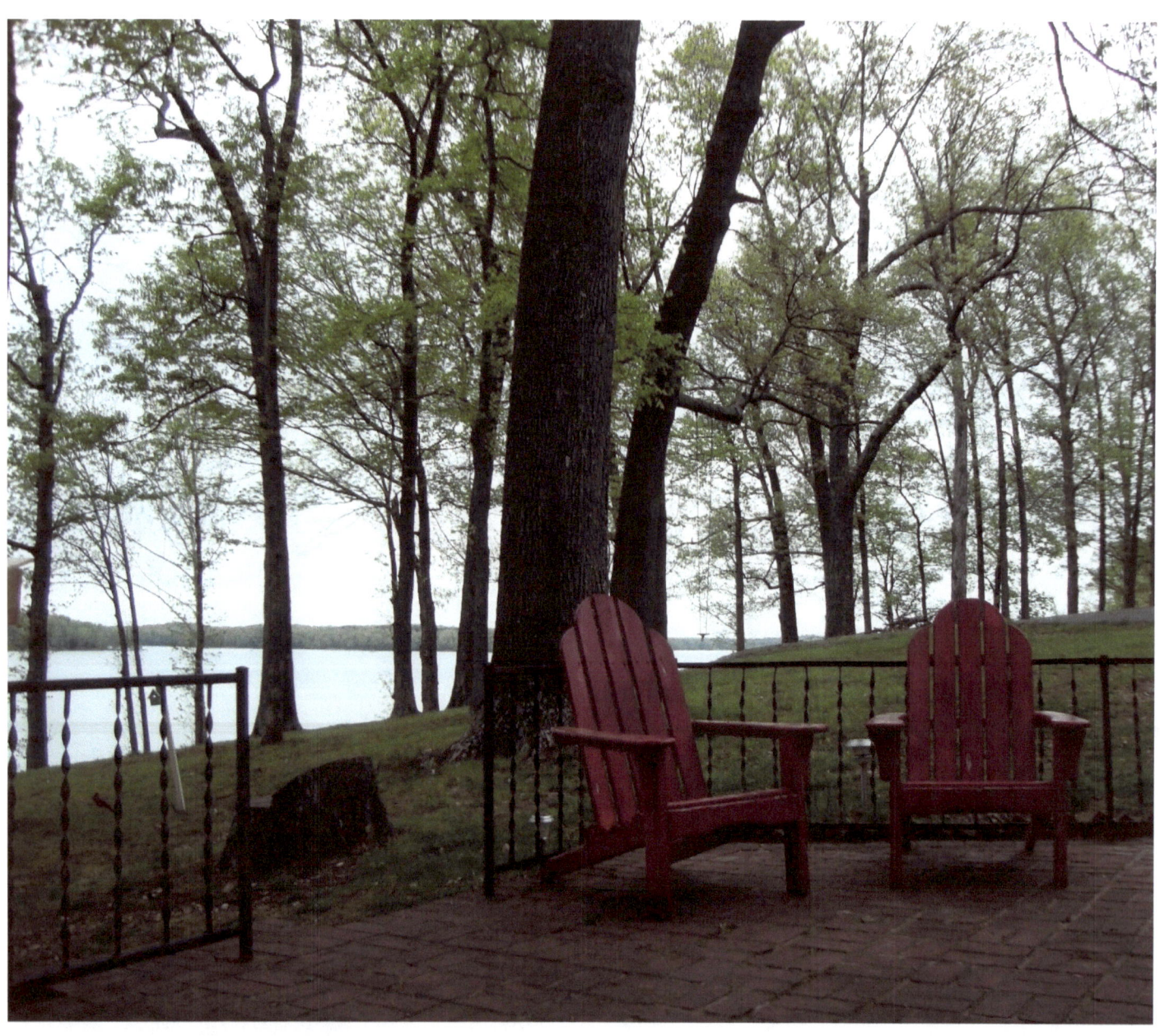

Come Sit With Me

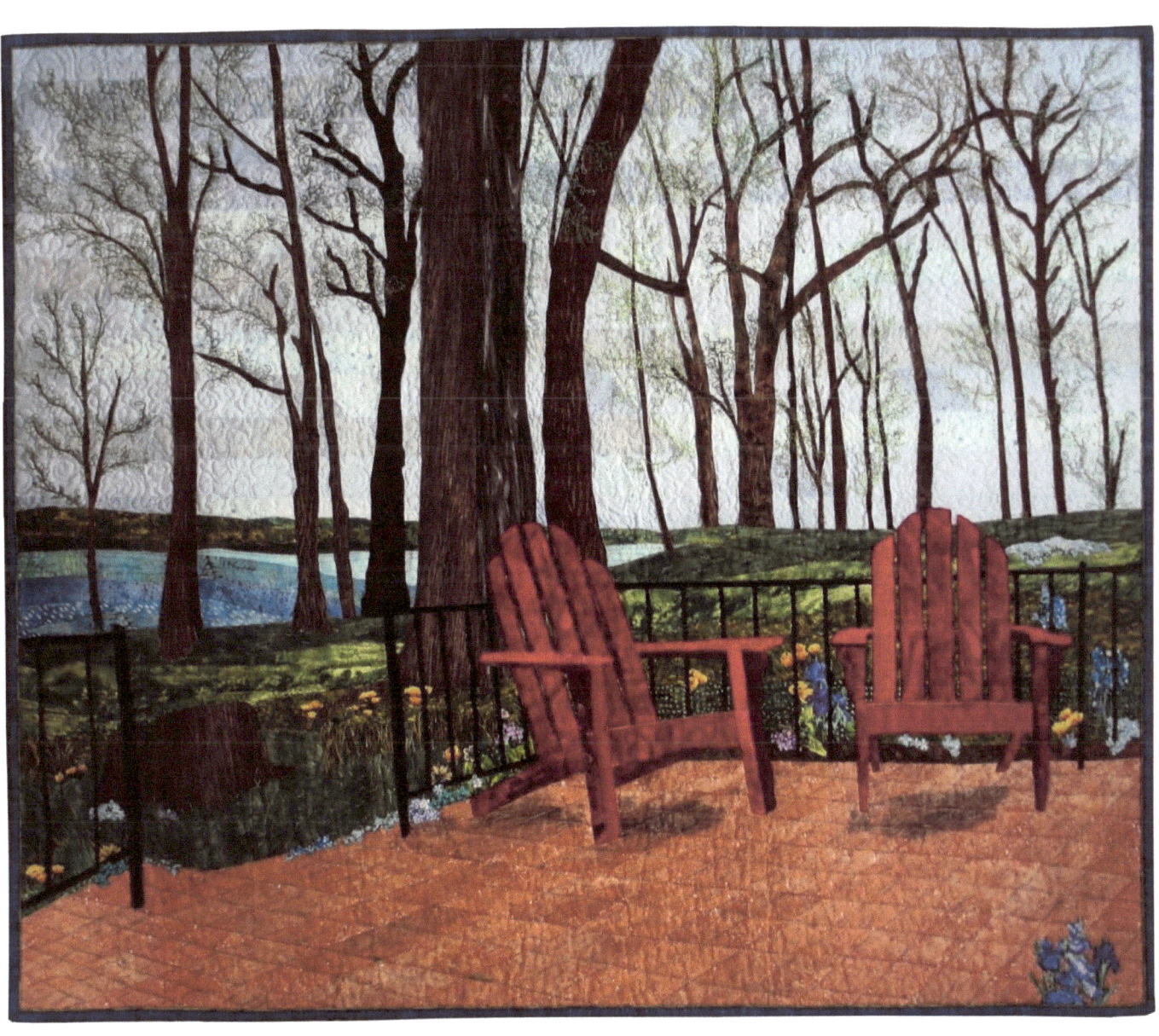

BESIDE THE STILL WATERS   88" x 44"

Water skiing, picnics, family fun--that's what I remember when I look at this quilt. I wanted to design a quilt of this location and had Gary photograph it for me. I combined 3 photos to get the width and have enjoyed sharing the quilt very much.

It really does "restore my soul" to look upon this peaceful place. Ps 23

Techniques: Background sky and water painted on white cloth, Mosaic picture piecing, and applique, tulle overlay on water, machine embroidery and quilting

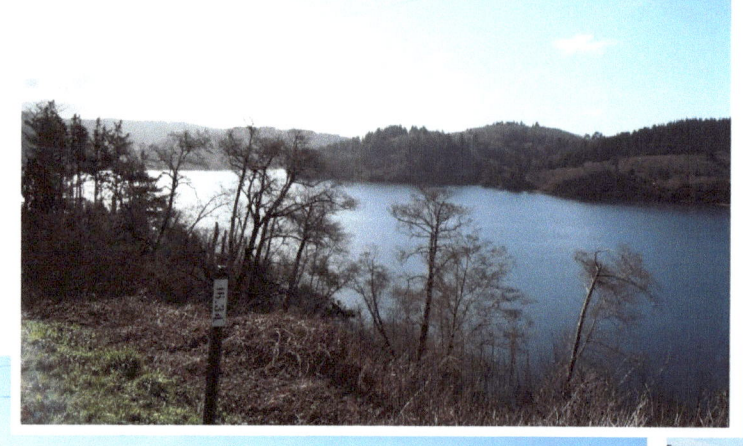

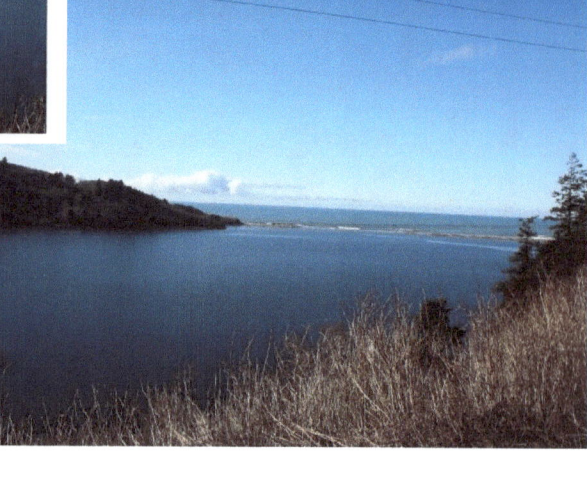

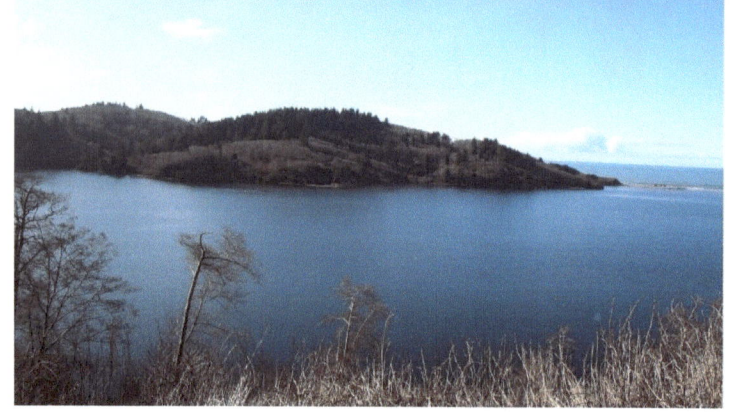

Inspiration photo Gary Durbin

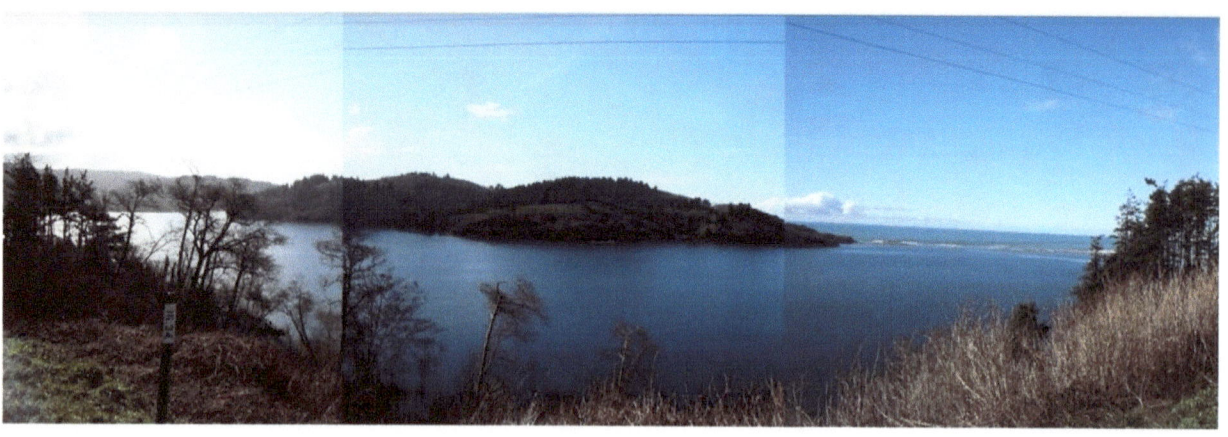

Beside the Still Waters

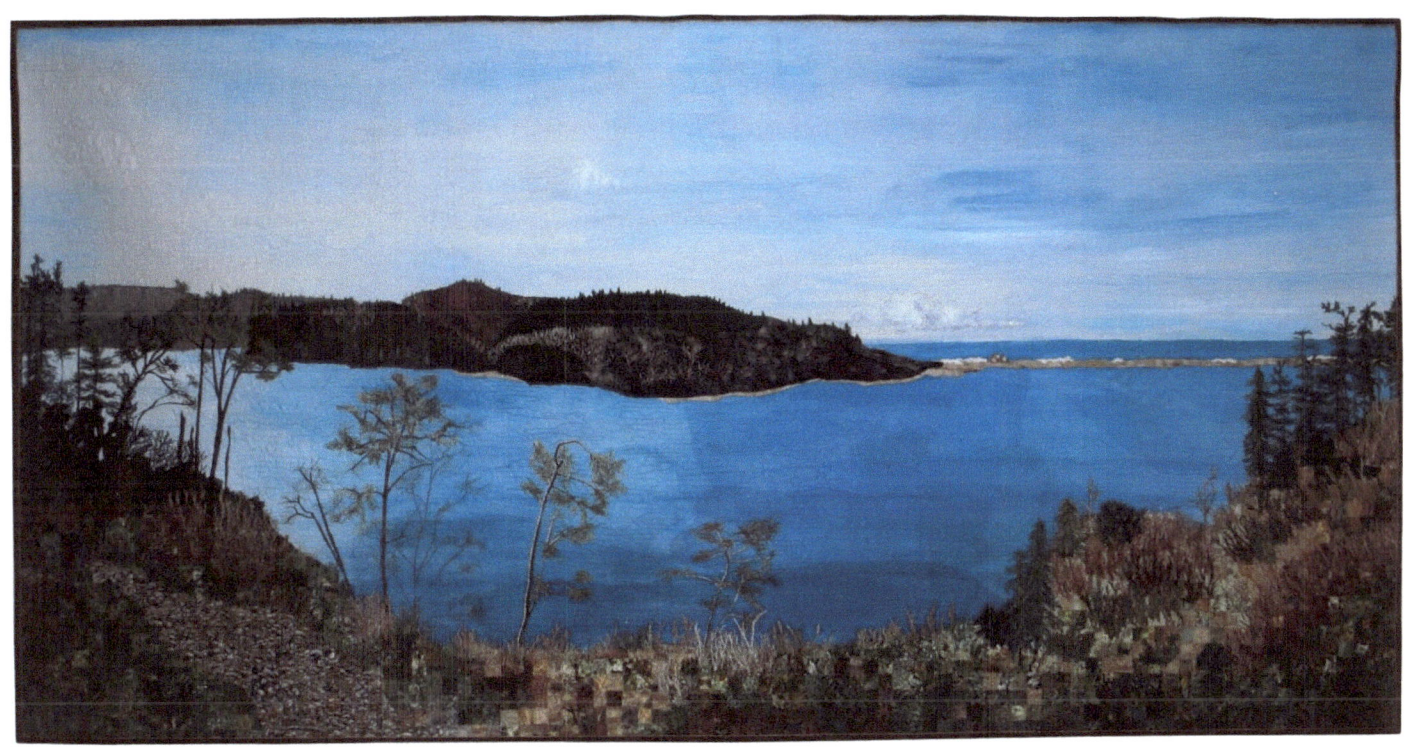

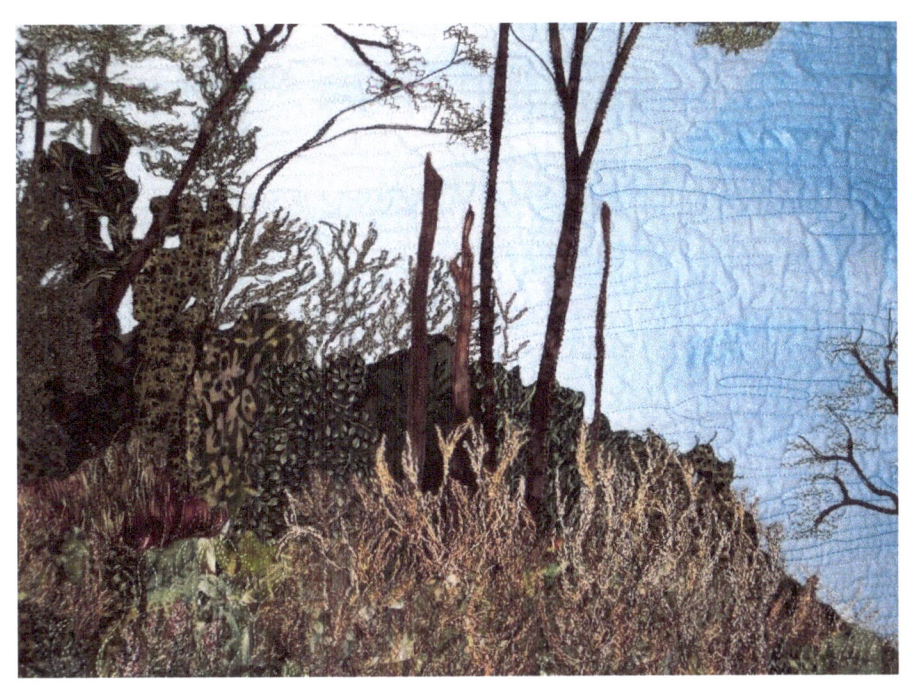

VANISHING HOMESTEAD 50" x 33"

Traveling, we crossed over the Columbia River near the Dows and traveled down through Oregon. Gary spotted this abandoned farm. We were fascinated by it because it looked like the family had just walked away. It felt kind of sad but beautiful.

Techniques: Painted whole cloth with heavy machine quilting.

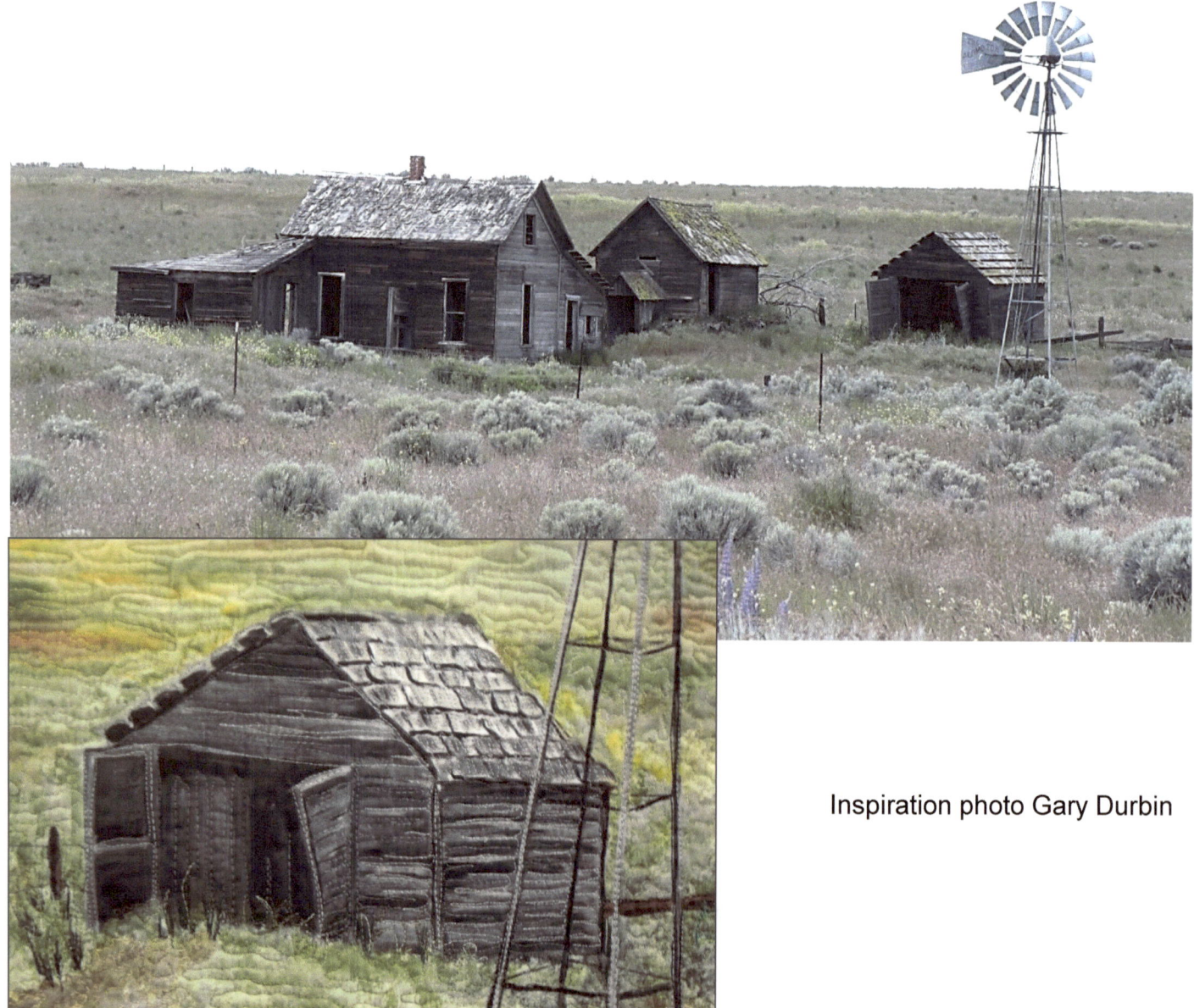

Inspiration photo Gary Durbin

Vanishing Homestead

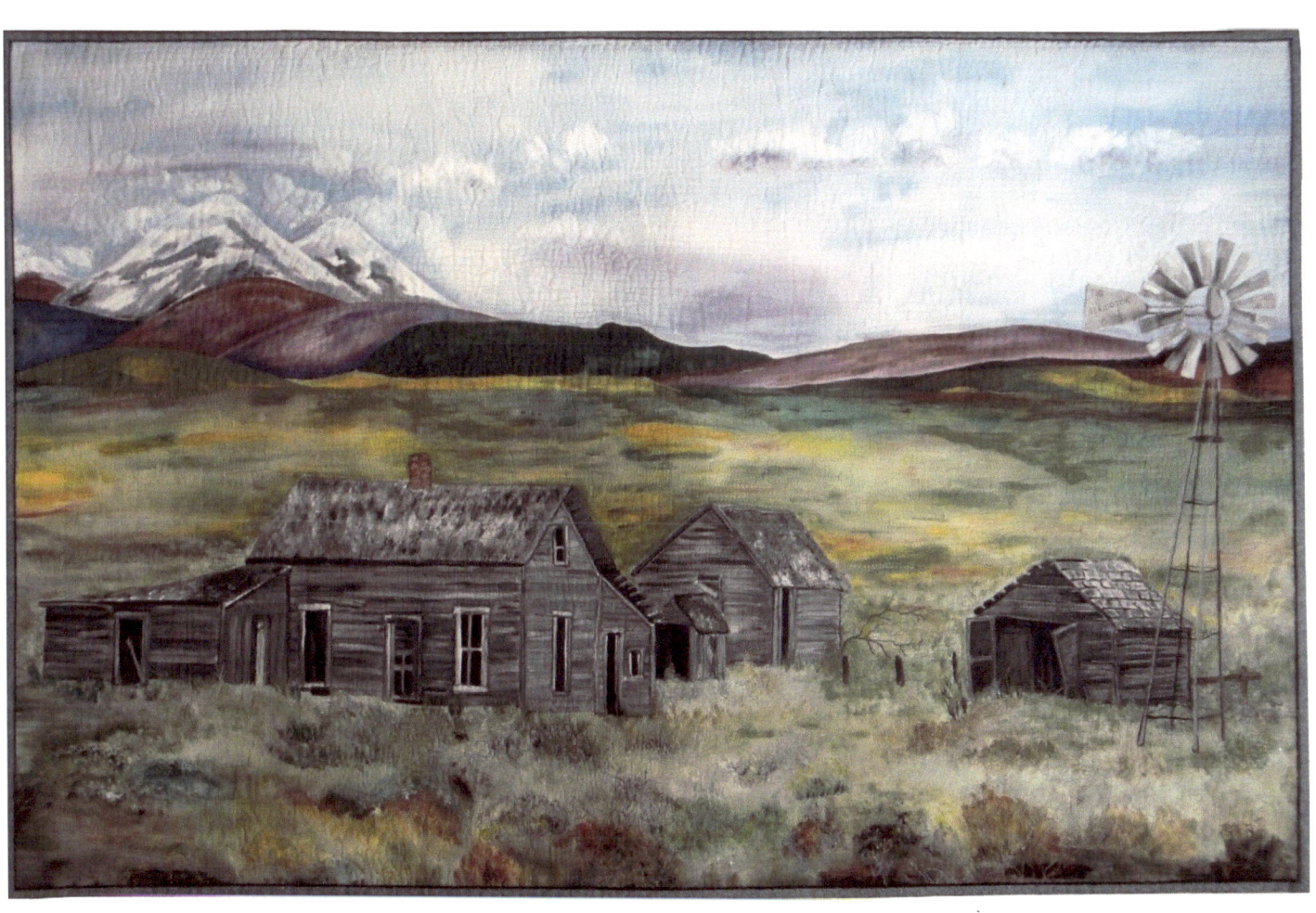

WILD RHODIES   35" x 65"

As you probably know I love the redwoods. Once a year in the forest you will also see wild rhododendrons scattered abroad. These red ones were such a beautiful contrast to the dark wood that they were my choice for a quilt.

Techniques: Mosaic piecing for background, applique, machine embroidery and quilting.

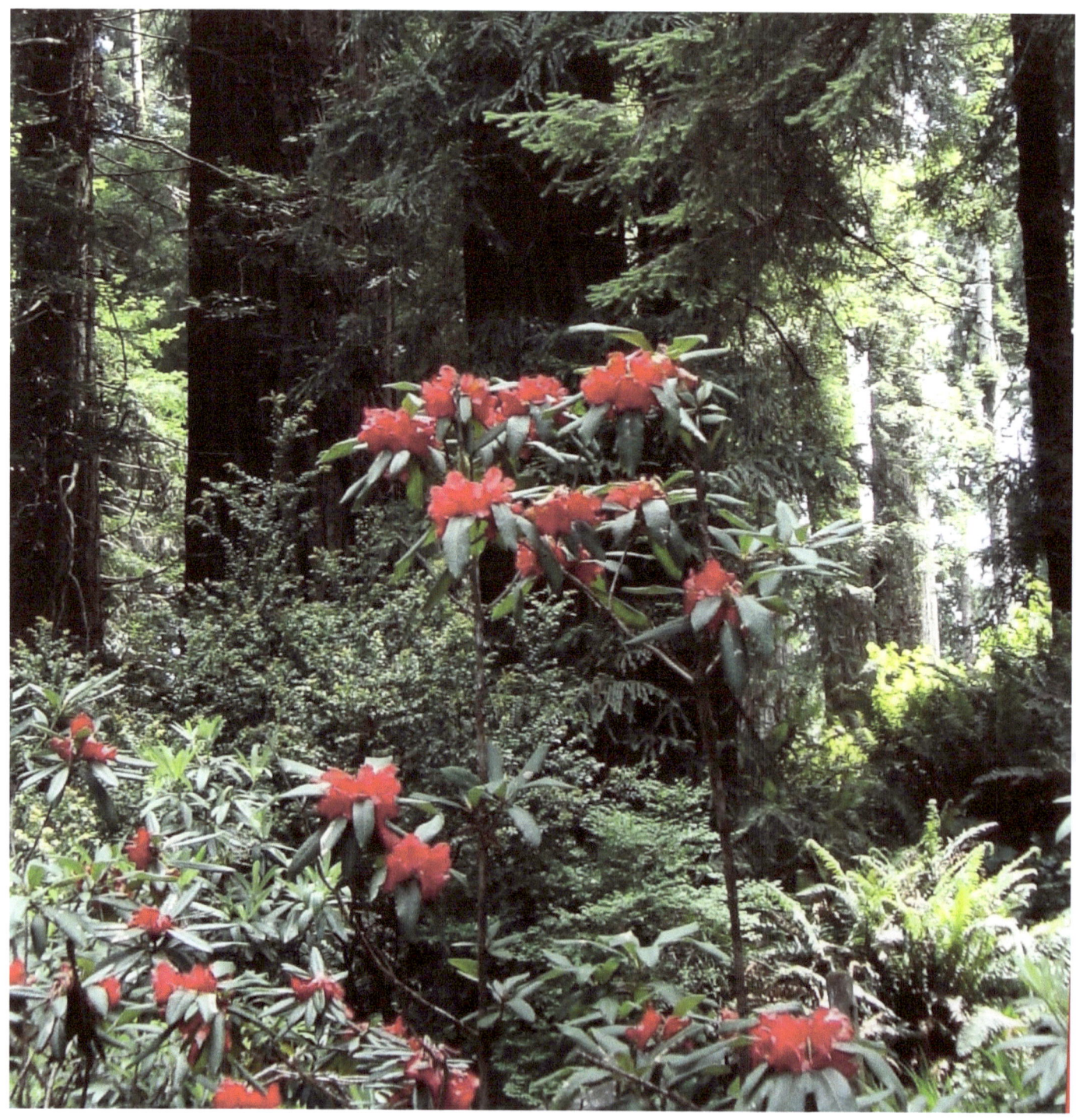

Wild Rhodies

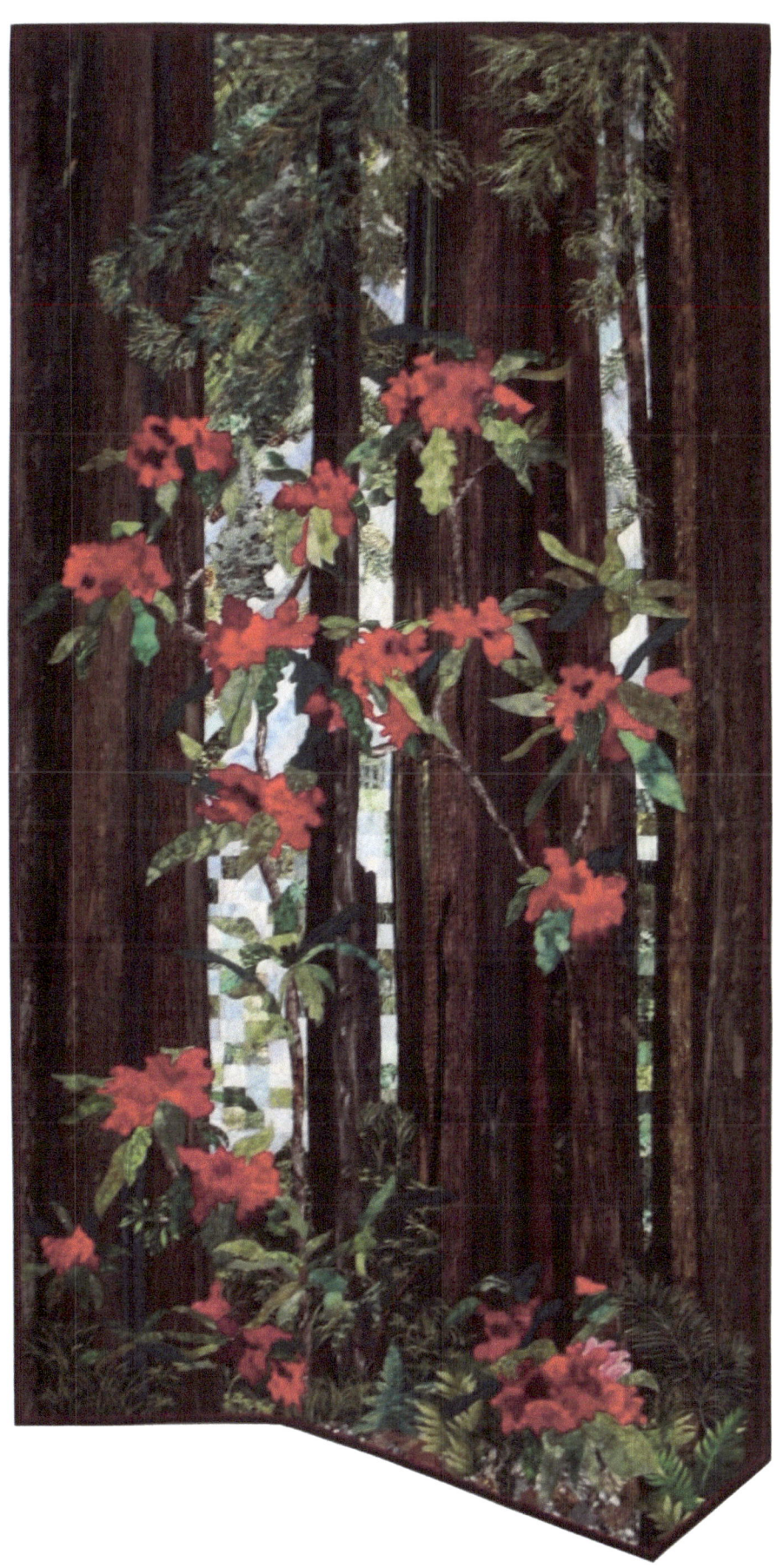

SMITH RIVER   34" x 29"

Smith River is beautiful. We drive by it when we travel to Oregon. It's a rocky bed with very clear water that rushes along parallel to the road. It's a view I've seen often through the years and always draws my eye.

Techniques: Mosaic picture piecing, freeform collage, machine quilted.

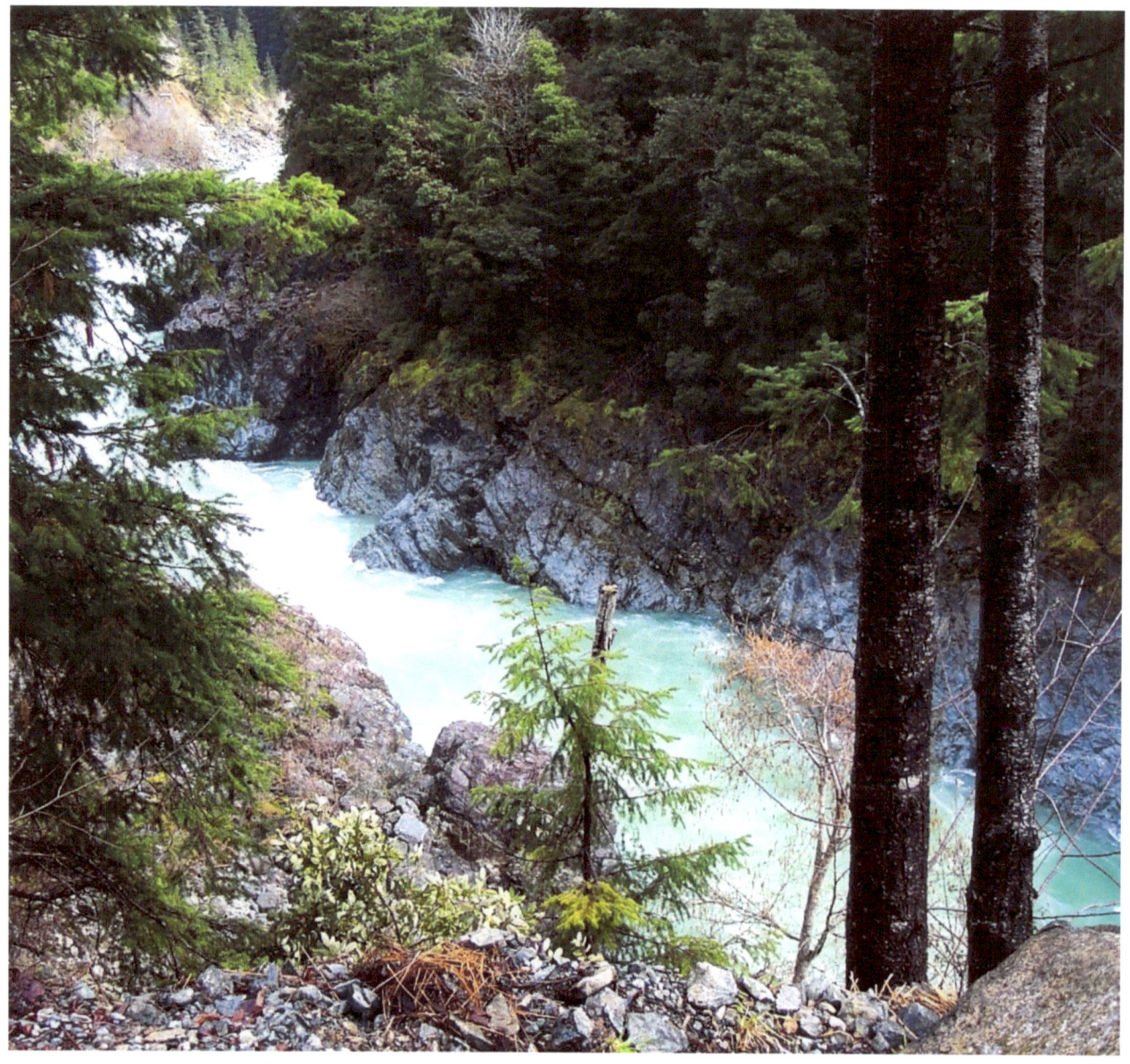

Inspiration photo Gary Durbin

Smith River

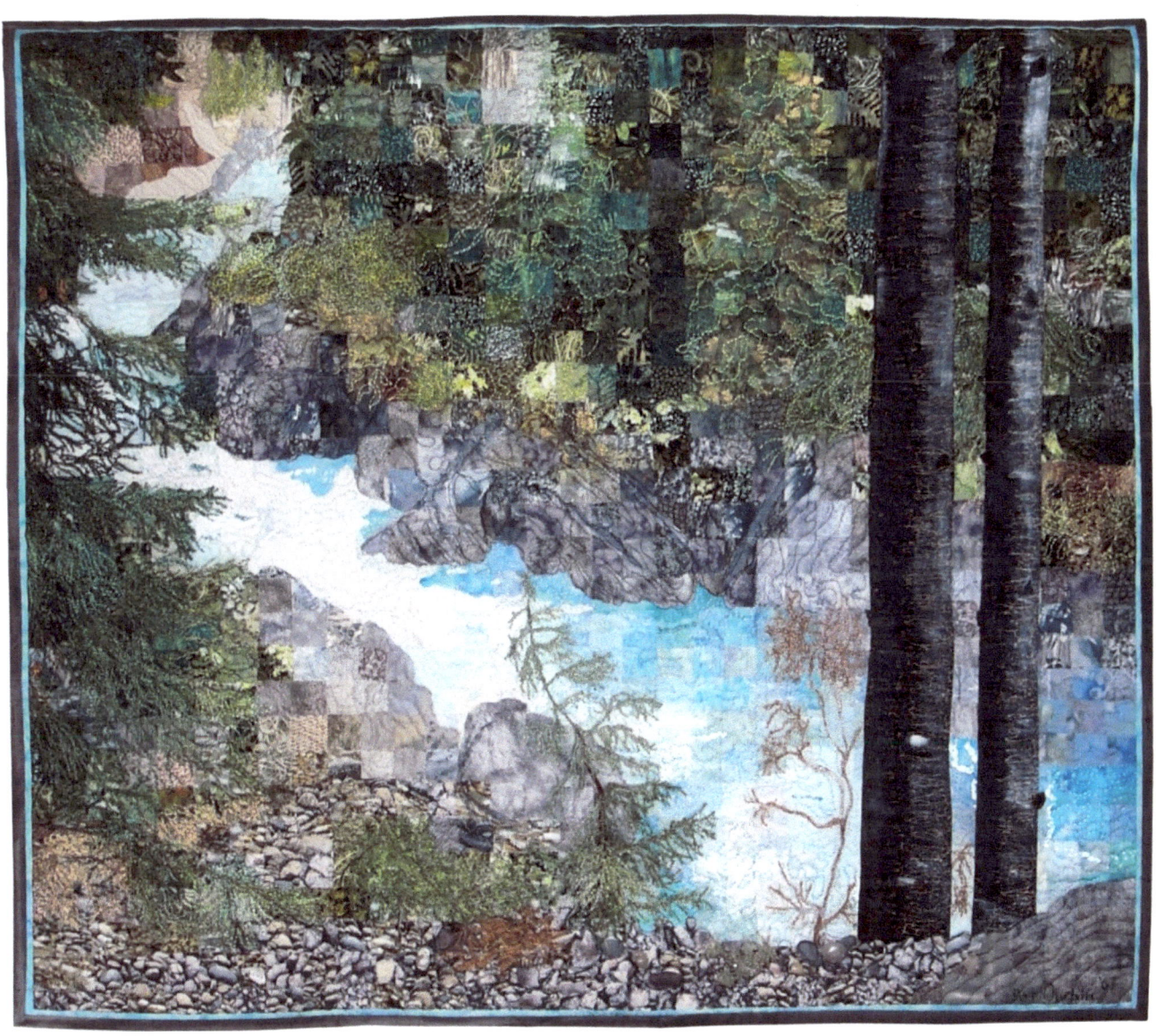

SUNLIGHT IN THE FOREST   65" x 58"

Light filtering through the tall dark trees just makes my heart glad. The forest is always beautiful, even in the fog, but this scene was very appealing because of the sunlight. In my mind these are redwoods, I'm not sure why all of those other leaves are hanging from them but it did add a variety and fun to the composition.

Techniques: Painted background and applique trees and foreground.

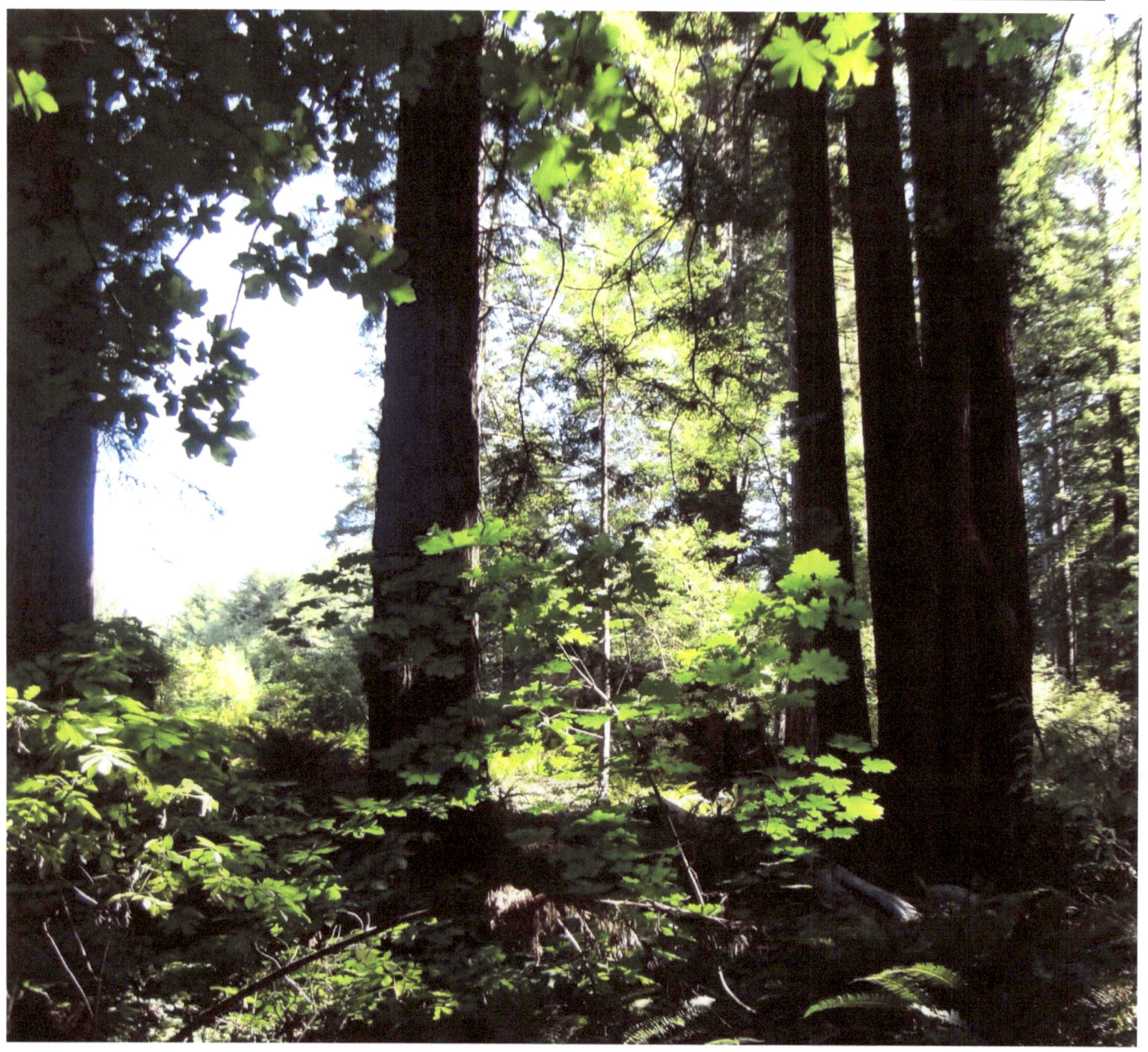

Inspiration photo Gary Durbin

Sunlight in the Forest

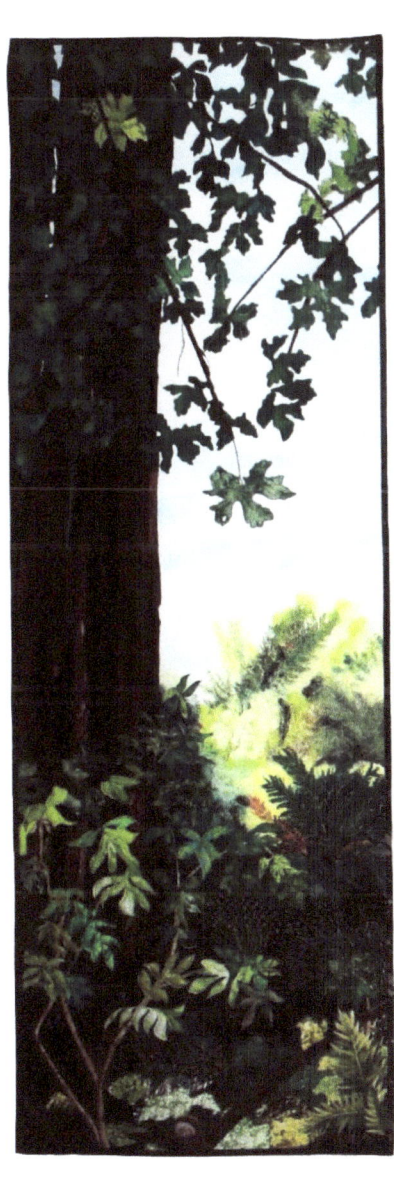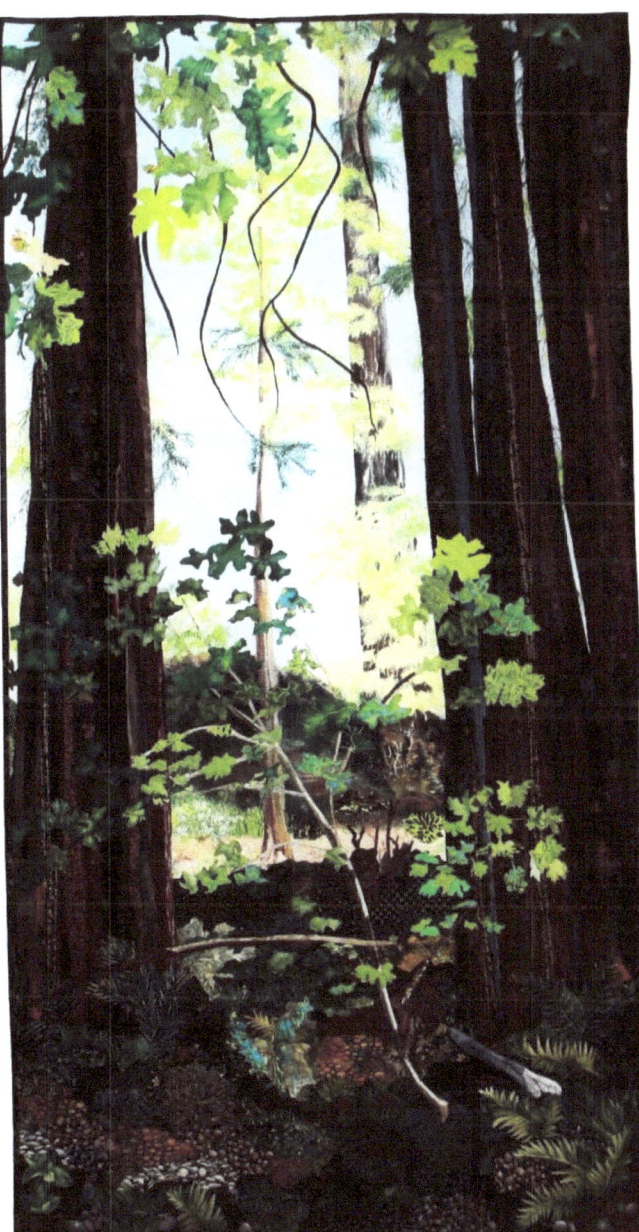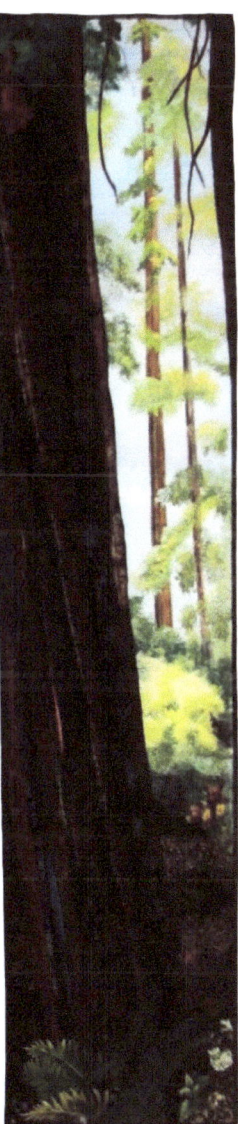

CLOUDY DAY AT HIDDEN LAKE   24" x 18"

Climbing up a steep incline outside of Steamboat Springs, Co. we decided to pull over and take some photos. (It seemed a bit treacherous to me.) However, this little jewel was the reward.

Techniques: Painted whole cloth, machine quilted.

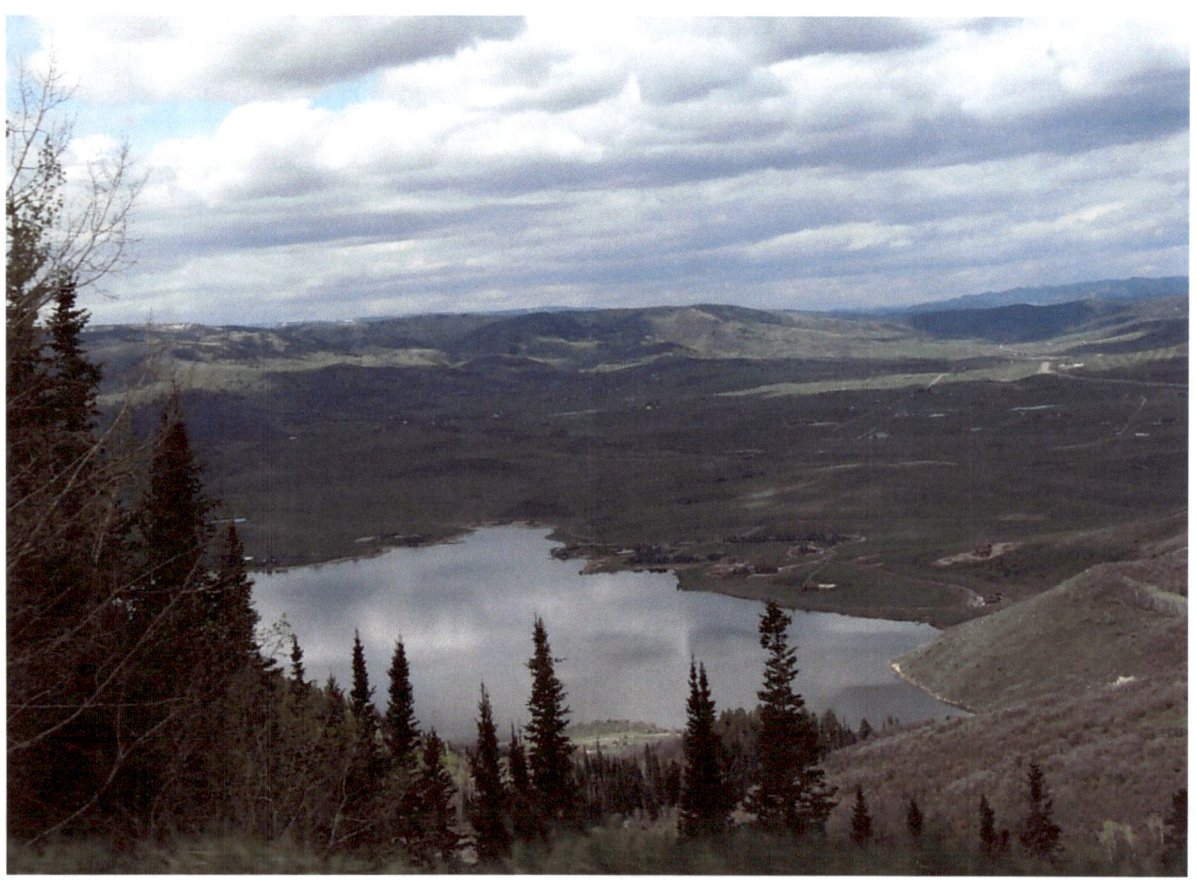

Inspiration photo Gary Durbin

Cloudy Day at Hidden Lake

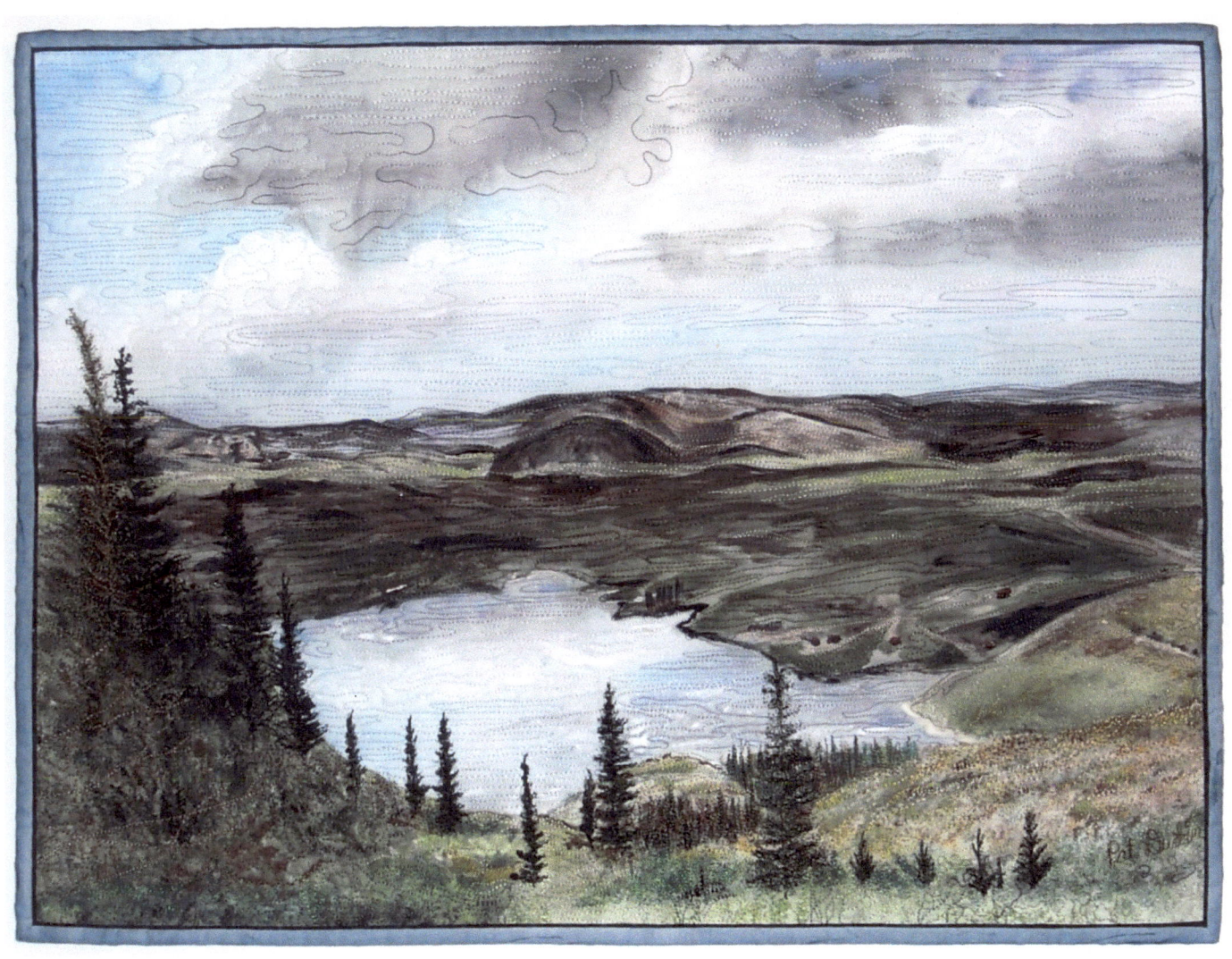

BEGONIA PICOTEE LACE   50" x 41"

One of my favorite flowers is a begonia. This fancy frilly flower with the red edges really caught my eye. I used some new techniques to showcase its beauty.

Techniques: Main image is painted on white cloth, applique edge, heavy thread painting and machine quilted

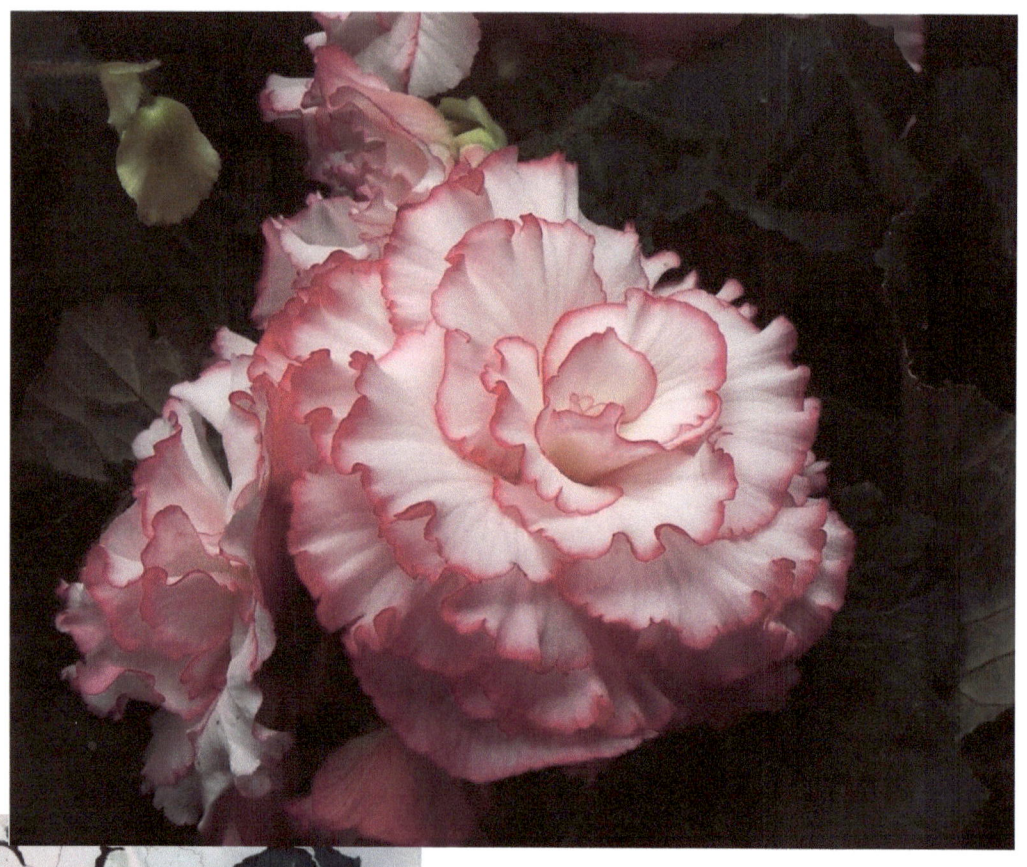

Inspiration photo Gary Durbin

Begonia Picotee Lace

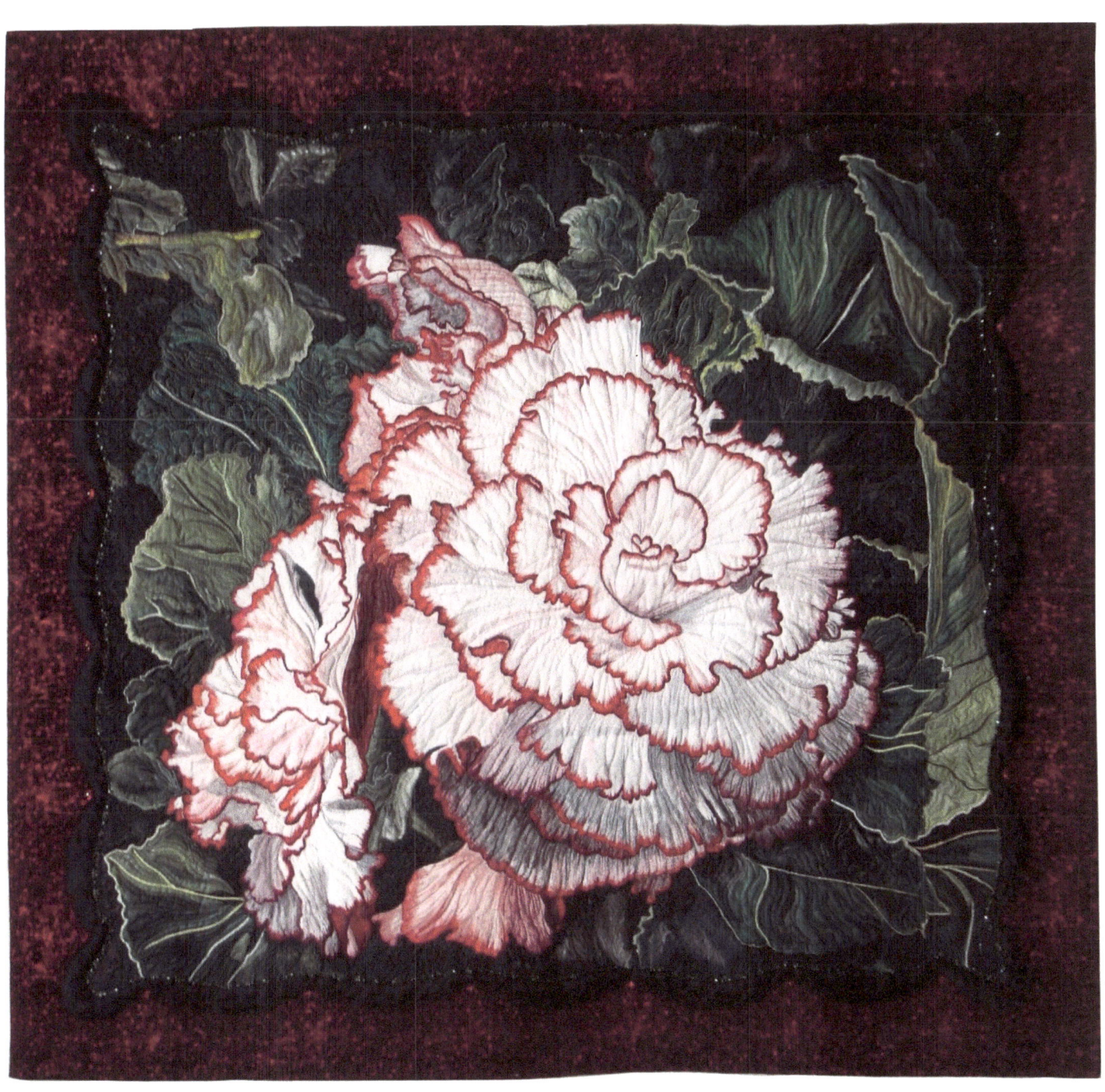

REST STOP   25" x 41"

This happy little scene caught my eye white we walked on the waterfront at Bandon Oregon. California poppies around this old fire plug just needed to be made into a quilt.

Techniques: Painted whole cloth, machine quilted.

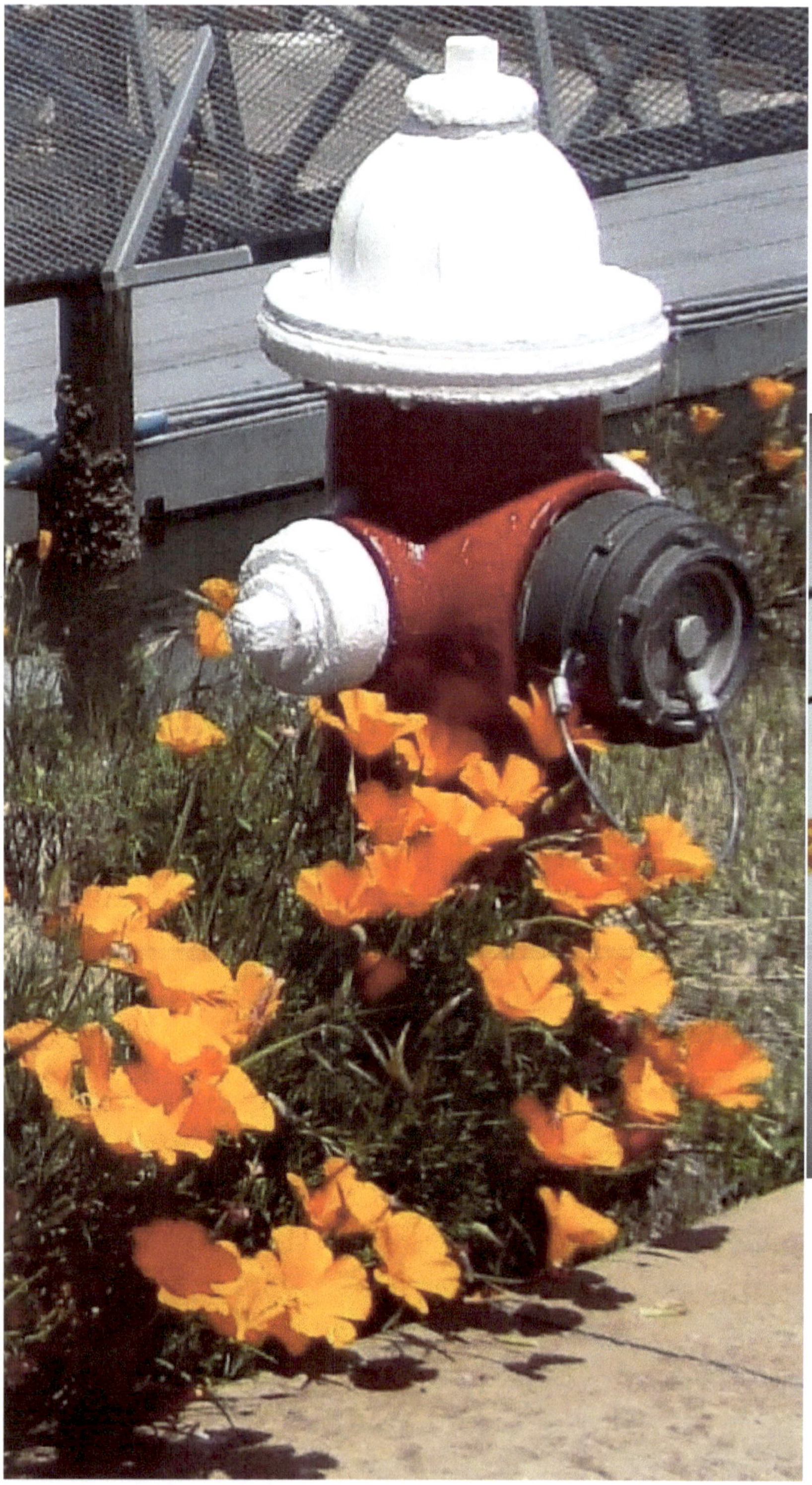

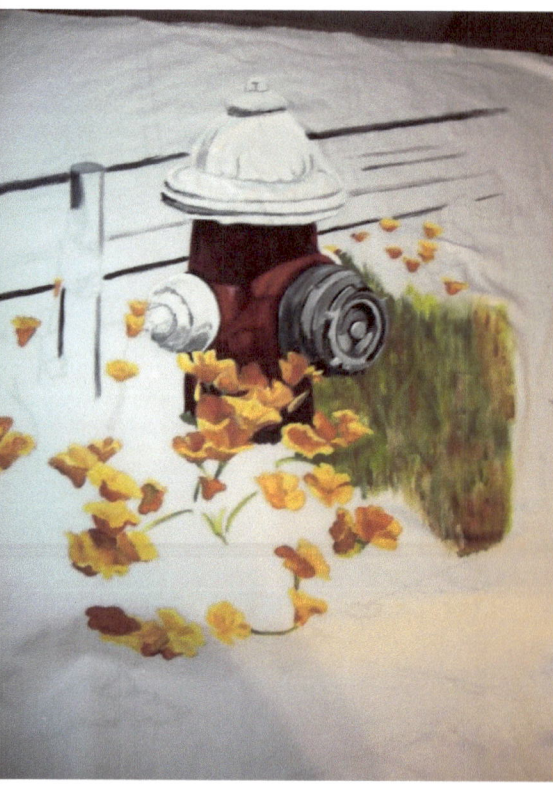

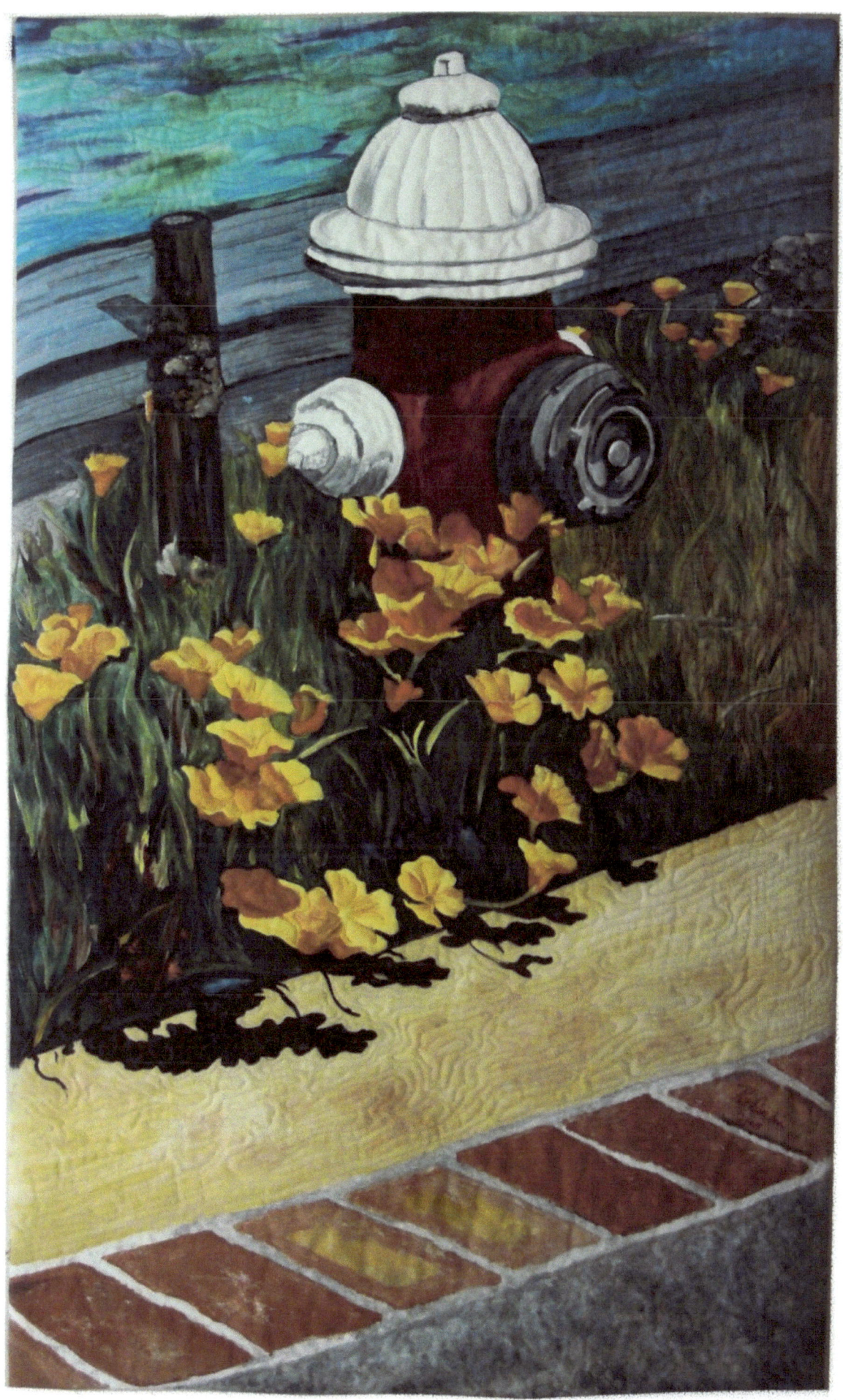

Rest Stop

COASTAL GARDEN	35" x 25"

Peeking over this flowered bush I caught a glimpse of the Pacific which added a bit of color and contrast.

Techniques: Mosaic picture piecing, Applique, machine quilted.

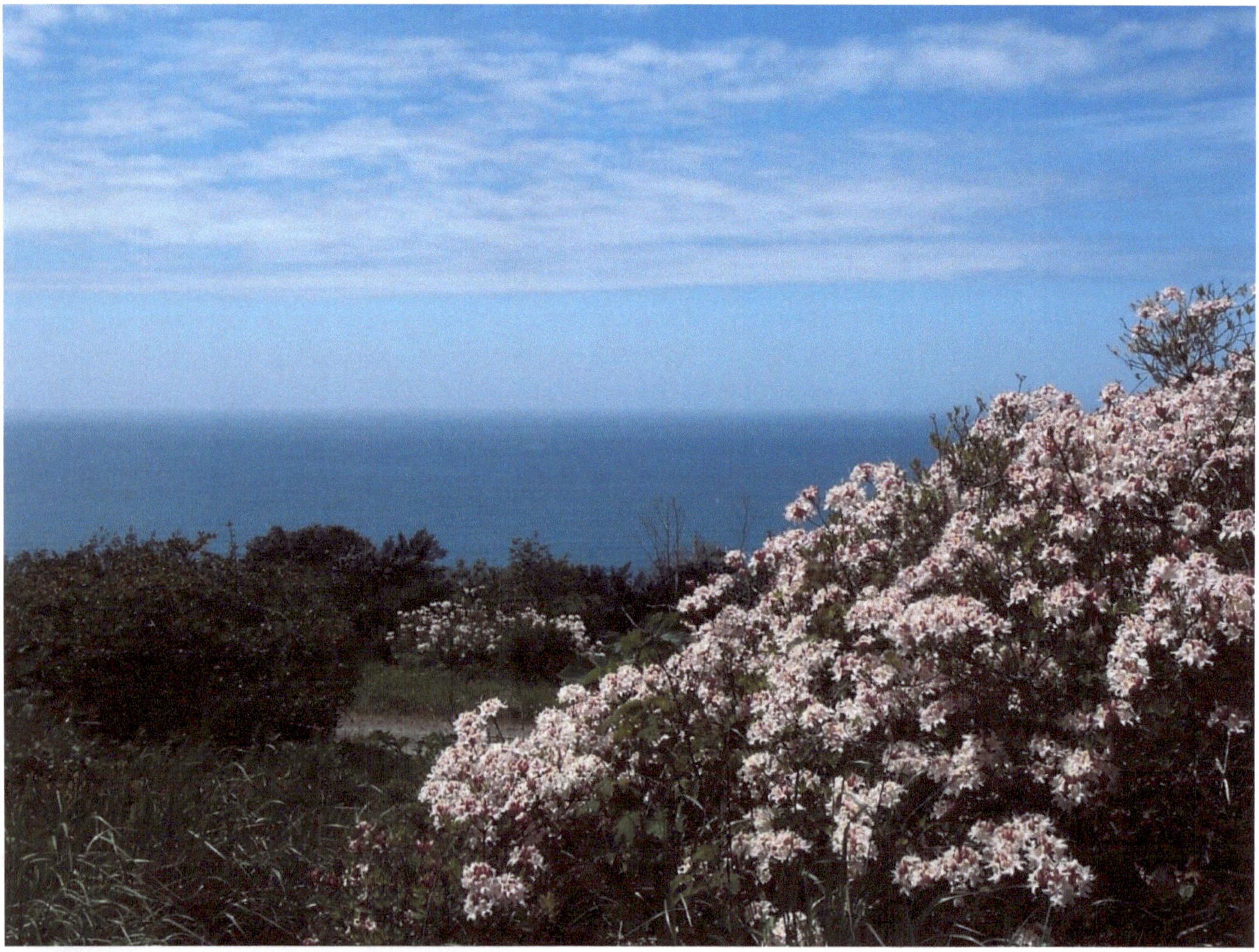

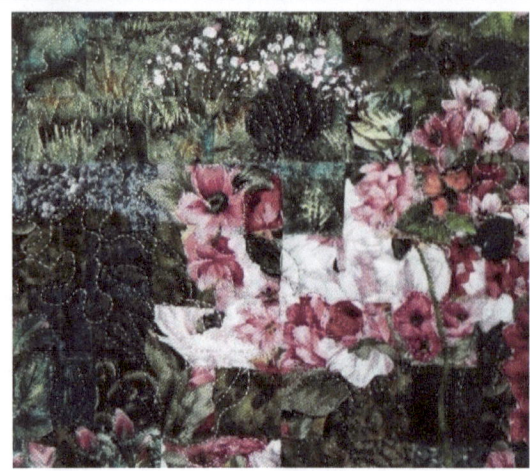

40

Coastal Garden

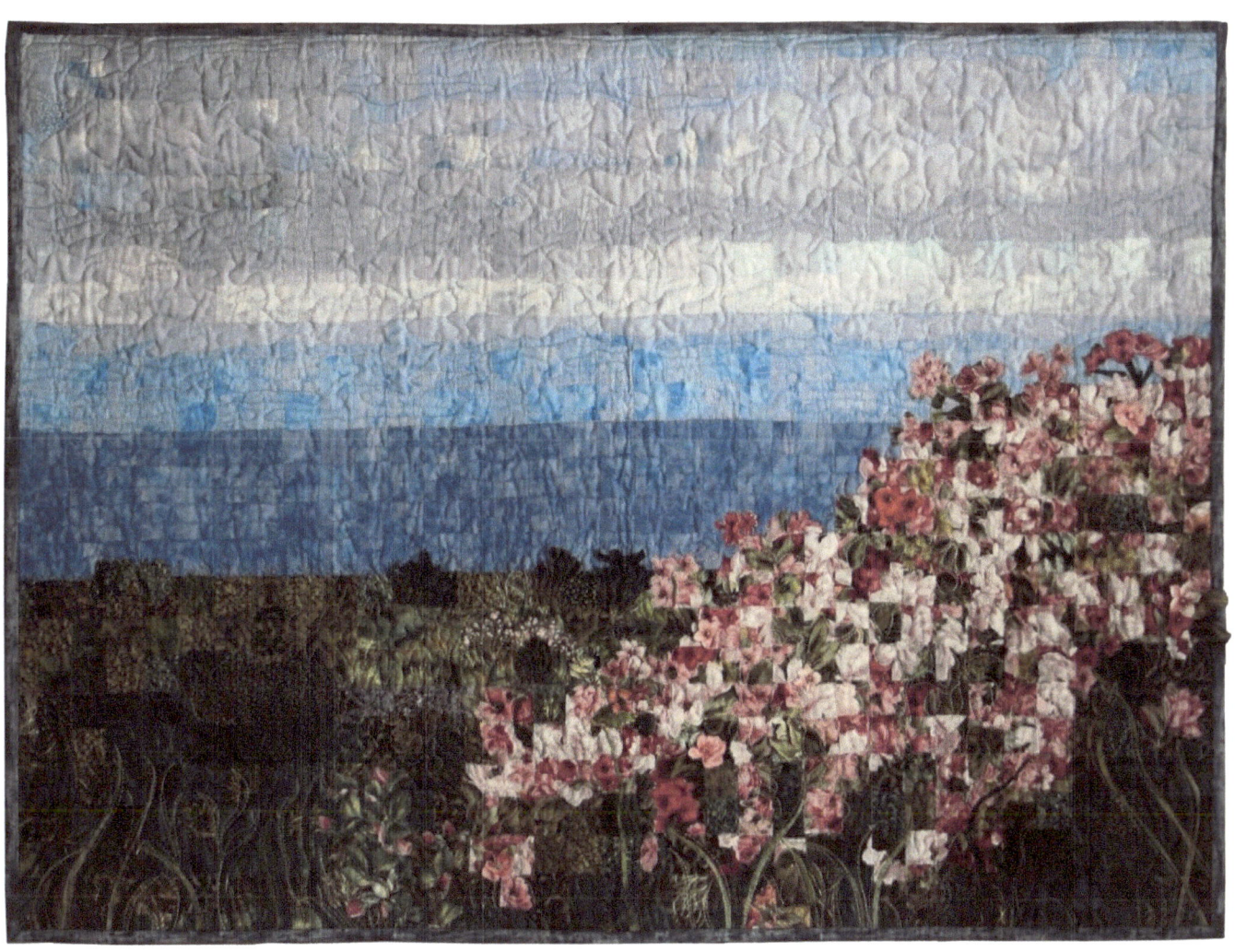

Meet the Durbins

Here we are doing what we do for fun. Gary has been an amateur photographer for a long time. He has become a major part of the artistic quilting that happens in and around our house.

Gary is a retired minister. He still enjoys many opportunities to preach the Gospel of Jesus.

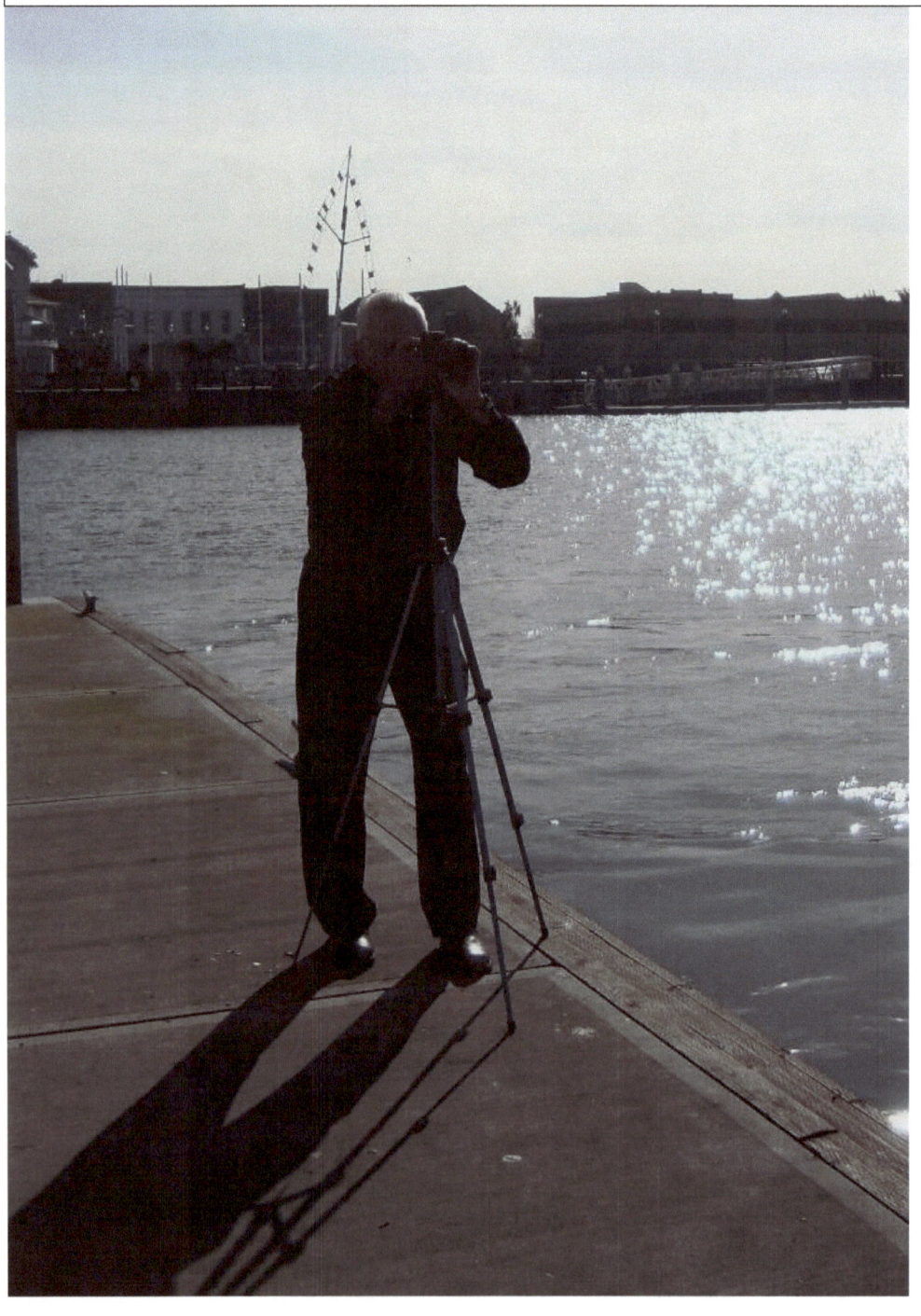

Pat is retired as well, but spends a lot of time quilting and working on related projects.

This is what you might see us doing if we're out and about or traveling. We're always looking for another great "shot".

We have many children, grand-children, and great-grandchildren who are a blessing in our lives.

We are thankful.

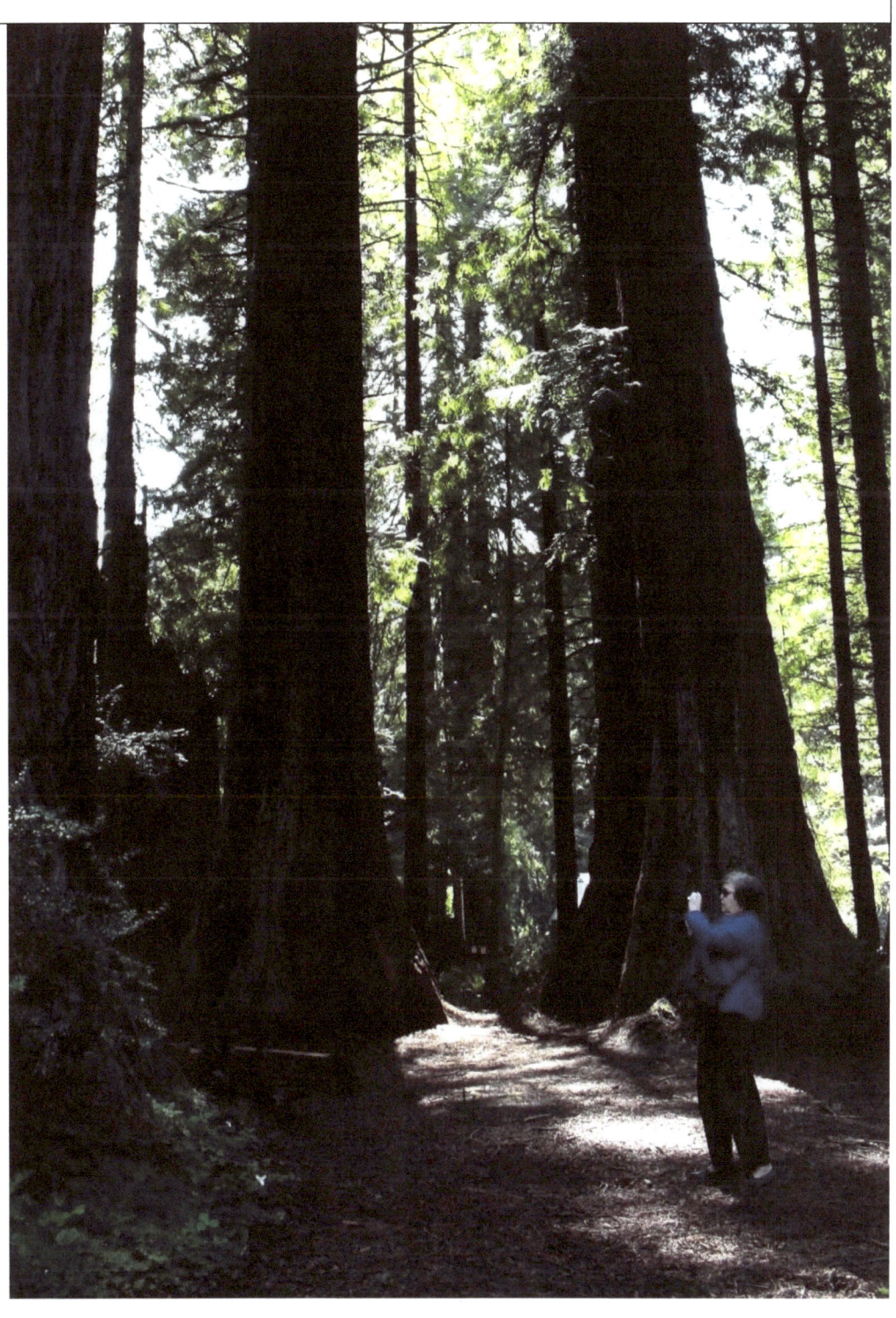

See more quilts on my website.

You'll also find some blogs and various items for sale.

Find It On the WEB www.patdurbin.com

Quilts

Patterns

Transparency Grids

Kits

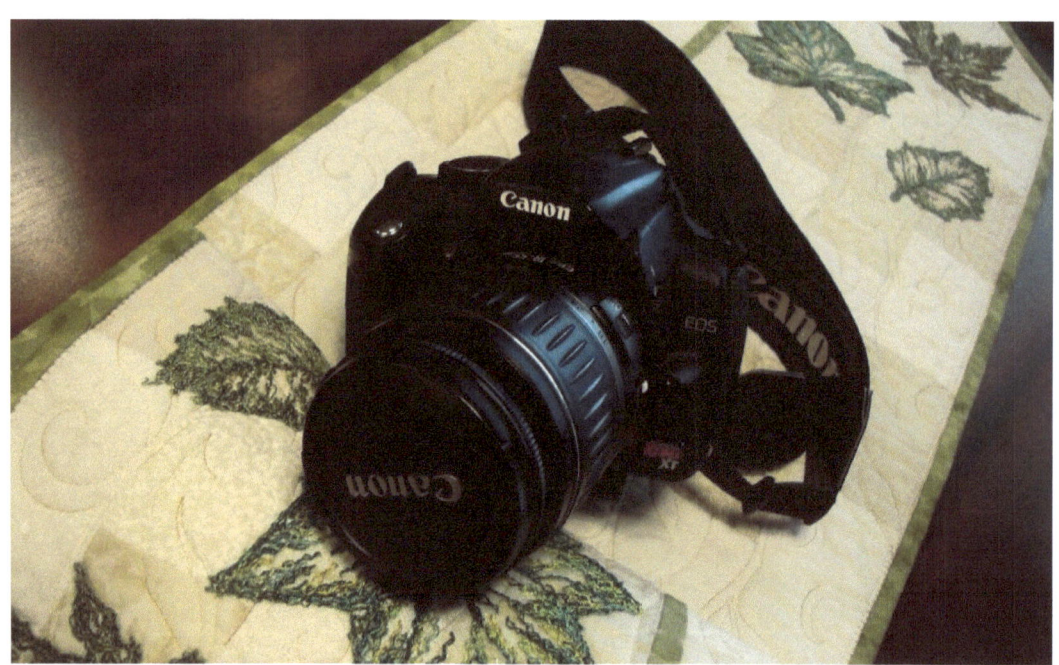

You may email me at stitching@suddenlink.net

Below you can see a variety of squares which will be used in the "Forest Walk" quilt. You can see part of a working sketch on the wall behind.

Many hundreds of squares go into making a mosaic quilt.

   Pat Durbin

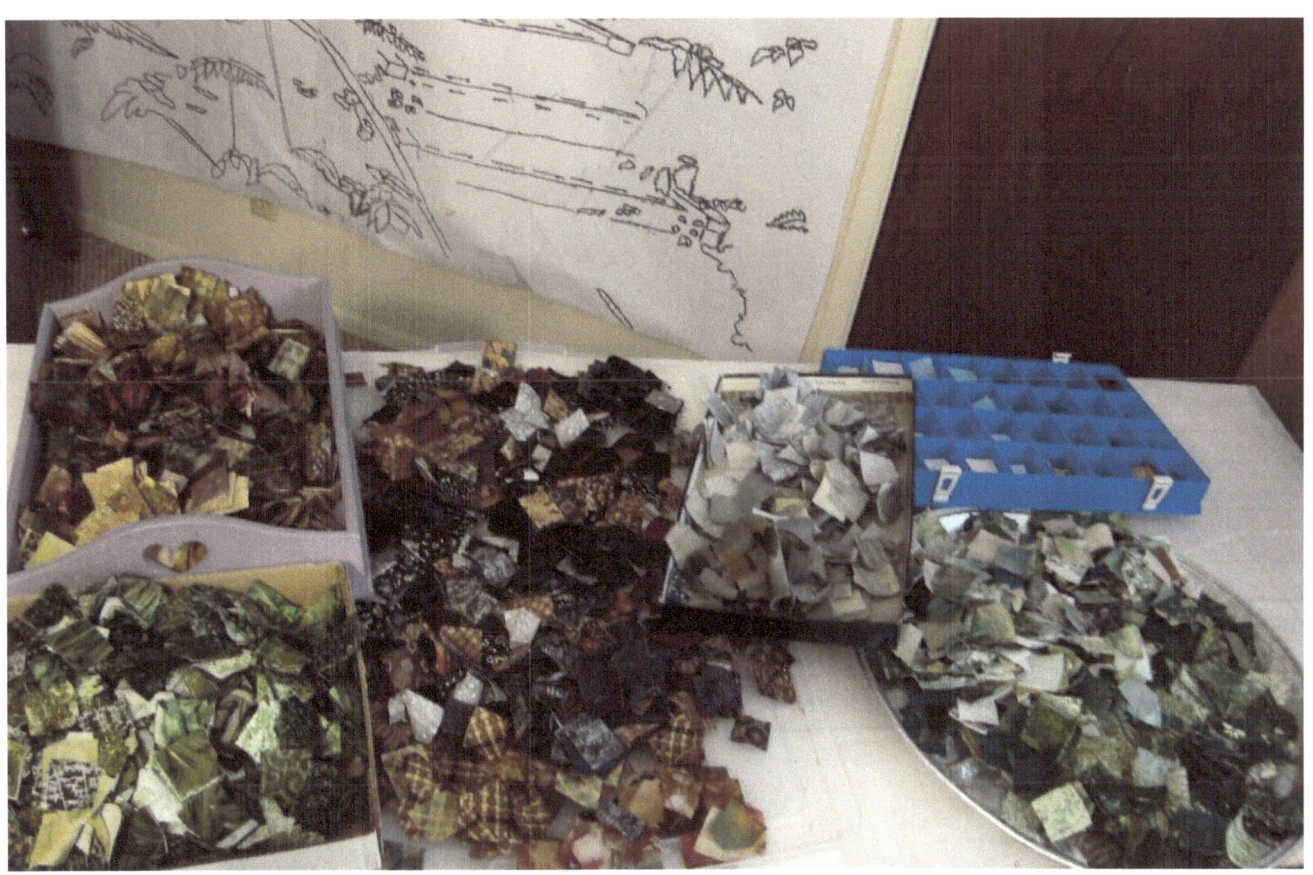